D0975527

You Have the Power

Also by Frances Moore Lappé

Hope's Edge: The Next Diet for a Small Planet
(with Anna Lappé)

Diet for a Small Planet

Food First: Beyond the Myth of Scarcity
(with Joseph Collins and Cary Fowler)

Mozambique and Tanzania: Asking the Big Questions
(with Adele Beccar-Varela)

Aid As Obstacle:
Twenty Questions About Our Foreign Aid and the Hungry
(with Joseph Collins and David Kinley)

Now We Can Speak (with Joseph Collins)

Nicaragua: What Difference Could a Revolution Make?
(with Joseph Collins and Paul Rice)

What to Do After You Turn Off the TV

World Hunger: Twelve Myths
(with Joseph Collins, Peter Rosset, and Luis Esparza)

Betraying the National Interest
(with Rachel Schurman and Kevin Danaher)

Rediscovering America's Values

Taking Population Seriously (with Rachel Schurman)

The Quickening of America:
Rebuilding Our Nation, Remaking Our Lives
(with Paul Martin Du Bois)

ear mean... n danger. Something's w... must esc... d seek safety. If I stop w... n doing, ...ost, I'll never start again. ve to ... ut before I can do any... act on ... believe, conflict will brea... be humili...d and ineffective. Our grea... ...rs are our worst enemies; they drag us...

You Have the Power

ear is pure energ... ...t's a signal. ...ght not mean s... ...t could m... ...! Sometimes... ...o stop ...der to fin... ...n't ... believ... ...ry act of sho... ...ven wit... ...r fear, has p... ...ict me... ...gagement. S... ...real is ... ...otio... ...clo... ...r worst fear... ...r grea... ...achers. To fir... ...conne... ...e must risk di... ...n. The... ...ht we shine ... ...rs tow... ...s, and we bec... ...ious ch... ...ery time we... ...ith ou...

Choosing
Courage in
a Culture
of Fear

Frances Moore Lappé and Jeffrey Perkins

JEREMY P. TARCHER/PENGUIN
a member of
Penguin Group (USA) Inc.
New York

Most Tarcher/Penguin books are available at special quantity discounts for bulk purchase for sales promotions, premiums, fund-raising, and educational needs. Special books or book excerpts also can be created to fit specific needs. For details, write Penguin Group (USA) Inc. Special Markets, 375 Hudson Street, New York, NY 10014.

While the authors have made every effort to provide accurate telephone numbers and Internet addresses at the time of publication, neither the publisher nor the authors assume any responsibility for errors, or for changes that occur after publication.

Jeremy P. Tarcher/Penguin
a member of
Penguin Group (USA) Inc.
375 Hudson Street
New York, NY 10014
www. penguin.com

Excerpt from *Letters to a Young Poet* by Rainer Maria Rilke, translated by Stephen Mitchell, copyright © 1984 by Stephen Mitchell. Used by permission of Random House, Inc.

Library of Congress Cataloging-in-Publication Data

Lappé, Frances Moore.
You have the power : choosing courage in a culture of fear /
Frances Moore Lappé & Jeffrey Perkins.
p.   cm.
Includes index.
ISBN 1-58542-312-2
1. Fear.   2. Courage.   3.Self-actualization (Psychology)
I. Perkins, Jeffrey, 1971-   II. Title
BF575.F2L37   2004   2003071156
179'.6—dc22

Printed in the United States of America
10   9   8   7   6   5   4   3   2   1

This book is printed on acid-free recycled paper. ∞ ○

Book design by Mauna Eichner

To all who helped create the
Center for Living Democracy (1990–2000)
in Brattleboro, Vermont,
without which we may never have met nor learned
crucial lessons about fear.
And to our alma mater,
Earlham College (Frankie '66, Jeff '94),
for encouraging us to engage with the world.

Contents

And if only we arrange our life in accordance with the principle which tells us that we must always trust in the difficult, then what now appears to us as the most alien will become our most intimate and trusted experience. How could we forget those ancient myths that stand at the beginning of all races, the myths about dragons that at the last moment are transformed into princesses? Perhaps all the dragons in our lives are princesses who are only waiting to see us act, just once, with beauty and courage. Perhaps everything that frightens us is, in its deepest essence, something helpless that wants our love.

—From *Letters to a Young Poet*,
RAINER MARIA RILKE[1]

Our Journey

frankie I never planned to write a book about fear, but every good teacher tells you to write about what you know. And several years ago, fear and I got well acquainted. The life I'd spent ten years building collapsed with a thunderous roar. Then, just when I felt most disoriented, most frozen by fear, my children threw me a perfect challenge: Return to the grounding of my youth, they said, "follow the food," as I did when I wrote *Diet for a Small Planet* in 1971. And, they added, we'll help.

Stirred with a new sense of mission, I leaped right into my fear. Writing what became *Hope's Edge: The Next Diet for a Small Planet*, I set out on a journey to five continents with my daughter and coauthor, Anna. Along the way, we met some of the planet's most extraordinary people, by all measures courageous; we learned a lot about courage—we learned it doesn't mean fearlessness.

Yes, fear is old and automatic and in our bones, but that's not the whole story. Having had such a close-up, visceral experience of fear myself, I was able to see its role far beyond my own private pain. I began to see how fear is not necessarily our protector. It can trap us into creating a world none of us wishes for or can long afford.

To write *Hope's Edge,* I had moved from a small Vermont town to Boston. It was my good fortune that a former colleague at the Center for Living Democracy in Vermont, Jeffrey Perkins, had moved here a few years earlier. Since Jeff was one of the very few people I knew here, of course I turned to this young man with whom I'd so enjoyed working to "bring democracy to life."

As Jeff and I sprinted toward this book's finish line, I had yet another curve in the road awaiting me, one of a woman's most dreaded fears. I was diagnosed with a rare breast carcinoma (fortunately, very treatable). Ultimately, I realize now, this shock helped me to complete our book, for daily I learned and relearned an essential truth: Fear and gratitude don't coexist easily in the same heart. I found that as I stayed centered in thankfulness for my many blessings—among them the opportunity to absorb and share the ideas you'll read here—my fear eased and my mind cleared. So the very process of writing this book became the living of its message.

jeff I arrived at Frankie's Center for Living Democracy fresh out of college and ready to take on the world. At the Center, I helped gather stories for its national news service, covering citizen problem solving. Our goal was spreading examples of bottom-up democracy. After two years I left to pursue a graduate degree in American Studies, seeking to understand how our culture has historically both inspired and thwarted citizen participation. I wanted to know why more Americans weren't jumping in to build a society closer to their values.

By the time Frankie arrived in Boston, I had come to see that there is only one force powerful enough to answer my question. That force is fear. My realization was influenced by my own recent experience with coming out as a gay man and by beginning to ask myself the biggest question of all: Why am I on this planet?

Both experiences deepened my respect for the power of fear. I began to see its role in stopping so many of us before we even get started. I also realized things didn't have to be this way; that we could turn our traditional view of fear on its head. Instead of seeing fear as a stop sign I began to see fear simply as a sign that I was moving into the unknown. I started telling myself, Fear means go! And soon I began to imagine what this shift might mean not only in our individual lives but for our communities and the planet.

I knew we had to begin by talking about fear, yet I also appreciated how tough that is. Most of us can talk about all sorts of personal things, but not fear. Wanting to share this new insight, I began leading Fear Means Go workshops through the Cambridge Center for Adult Education. With Frankie new to the city, we started talking, too. With each other, there was no way to hide our fear; we didn't try.

Later, as Frankie traveled to dozens of cities to share stories from *Hope's Edge,* my hunch was confirmed. She would call me from the road—whether in San Antonio, San Francisco, or Seattle—and tell me that an almost palpable sigh of relief would sweep the room when she spoke about fear. After each talk, countless people would approach her, saying, "Thank you for talking about fear."

At the same time, I was beginning to build a community of people seeking ways to chart their unique paths in the world. As I listened to my friends tell me how fear kept them from their hopes for themselves and the world, I realized I had tapped in to something much bigger than I'd ever imagined.

we This book was born in the long heart-to-hearts we shared—in coffee shops and on long walks during Frankie's first dark, cold months in Cambridge. It

took shape through conversations with dozens of people across the country and around the world. It is a journey to see fear differently, for we have come to believe that we each can let go of our culture's limiting ideas about fear that hang heavily in the air—dangerous ideas that block our free expression, thwart our happiness, and threaten our planet. We can replace them with new, freeing ideas.

While our book is highly personal, it's not a how-to book, for there are no one-two-three-and-you're-there approaches to transforming our experience of fear. The journey is unique to each of us, and it is lifelong. This walk, we've also learned, is definitely not a straight line, nor evenly paced. It's a zigzag. Midway through this book, we became so afraid that we canned the idea before rediscovering its essential message: that fear can mean *go*, not stop.

In these pages, we share our own journeys as well as those of people we have met far and wide, from a young Sikh-American at Stanford to a Cambodian survivor of Pol Pot, from a dentist in Pittsburgh to a fourth-generation shrimper in the Gulf of Mexico. We ask you to entertain the surprising notion that fear—that oldest of all bogeymen—may be a precious resource we can use to create the lives we want and the world we want.

Seven Swordsmen
at the Door

One spring day not long ago, the two of us hailed a cab in Boston. Noting the driver's strong Russian accent, Frankie asked, "So what do you think of America?"

Hesitant at first, he finally blurted out, "You Americans are all afraid."

As we approached Harvard Square, two BMWs passed us. "Those people are the most afraid," the driver said, gesturing at the cars. "They're afraid they'll lose it. In Russia, we feared the KGB. Here, you don't trust anyone. You're all afraid of each other."

We climbed out of the cab shaking our heads, for the philosopher behind the wheel that morning had seemed to peer right into the heart of our nerve-jangled nation. A terror-alert system that never drops below yellow reminds us that in this new "permanent war," we can expect attacks at any moment. Hospital entrances now sternly warn: "Do not enter if exposed to anthrax." (As if we'd even know!) Potential killers of every shape and size swarm around us: airplanes, errant asteroids, ozone holes, and possible poison gas—got your breathing mask and duct tape?

At the same time, unexpected layoffs, vaporizing retirements, and a staggering national deficit all conspire to make us feel that we're just one pink slip away from being deluged in debt, losing our homes, our futures.

And speaking out against these assaults? Well, how safe is that in an era when someone can get arrested in a mall—as actually happened in upstate New York—for wearing a "Give peace a chance" T-shirt?

As the ground under us—the ground of personal security, fairness, and even common sense—seems to be slipping away, the fear in our bellies shouts out: Stop! Retreat! Pull back and take no risks. We can feel like rabbits frozen still in the grass, believing that if we just duck into the trenches of our private lives, going along and keeping quiet, we'll be invisible and safe. Well, maybe not safe, but at least as safe as we can be in this scary world.

Only there's one big problem: Living in fear, trapped by it, robs us of life. Human beings weren't made for this state; we evolved for something better, much better. We Homo sapiens never would have made it to six billion if we were not by nature curious problem solvers, actors, creators, beings who love to take risks, to live exuberantly, to aspire to what is beyond easy reach.

But so many of us feel stuck.

We're bewildered, unable to grasp how it could be that humans are creating a world none of us desires. After all, not one of us got up this morning saying, Yes, my goal is to make sure that one more young child dies of hunger; yet today almost sixteen thousand will.[2] Not one of us turned off the alarm in order to plot how best to spoil the environment; yet almost two hundred Americans will die today from the air we breathe.[3] Not one of us arose yearning for violence to escalate; yet the last one hundred years have been by far the bloodiest in human history.[4]

Our world is slipping increasingly out of whack with our common dreams—for one reason. We believe we don't have the power to create anything else, to create the lives and the world we really want. What lies at the root of this acquiescence? Why on earth do we go along?

Fear. It is fear that stops us.

For many, it's the fear of being different, of standing

apart from others if we refuse to go along. And it's the fear of that unknown land we'd be entering if we were to listen to our hearts and our own common sense.

So if fear is simply a hardwired response, we *are* powerless. These two fears, of the unknown and of being different, seem to congeal into the bedrock that maintains the status quo. But through our own experiences with fear and those of the people you'll meet in this book, we've come to see that it is our *ideas about fear* that are all important. They can shut us down, or they can allow us to discover our power to create the lives and the world we want.

Before exploring this startling discovery, we must grasp how fear is being fomented today—how we're made to breathe it in.

Consider George W. Bush's speeches surrounding the Iraq war. Sometimes his words have been downright chilling: "At some point we may be the only ones left," he said shortly before launching the attack, and "that's okay with me."[5] In another speech during that tense time, Bush made forty-four consecutive statements referring to the crisis and future catastrophic repercussions—a major presidential swing toward fear-inducing rhetoric, according to analyst Renana Brooks, even when compared to

Ronald Reagan.[6] And that's saying a lot! After all, it was Reagan who, while running for office, told us that "We may be the generation that sees Armageddon."[7] (Hearing such rhetoric, it's easy to ignore measures suggesting that the world is actually getting *less* dangerous, according to Joseph Cirincione of the Carnegie Endowment for International Peace.[8] Fewer nuclear weapons dot the planet today than fifteen years ago, he notes, as well as fewer biological and chemical weapons, even fewer missile-delivery systems.)

We feel more vulnerable not just because government leaders lay on the frightening language. We're also hit daily with scary media messages, from news images of escalating violence in the world's hot spots to advertisers playing on our fears of everything from crow's-feet to crime.

SUV makers design their stunningly successful marketing to convince us we need their industrial-strength protection on wheels to survive a hostile (and distinctly feminine) Mother Nature and to fend off dangers lurking on inner-city streets.[9] One market researcher described SUVs as: "armored cars for the battlefield. . . . Even going to the supermarket you have to be ready to fight."[10] SUV designs themselves speak of fear. Following the lead of the Dodge Ram, SUV makers developed more "menacing front ends" and fenders reminiscent of a "strong animal" with a "big jaw."[11]

Media distortions also heighten our dread. Even as rates of violent crime have diminished, media coverage of crime hasn't eased up—in fact, it has gone up. Homicide network-news coverage from 1990 to 1998 leaped almost sixfold (not even counting the O. J. Simpson trial), though the actual murder rate over this period fell by 20 percent.[12] No surprise, then, that by the mid-1990s, two-thirds of Americans described themselves as "truly desperate about crime," almost twice as many as in the late 1980s, when crime was worse.[13]

Doubly troubling is what gets lost in all the fear hype: the actual threats to our well-being, which we could and should do something about—right now. Think of the global warming (more fittingly called climate chaos) that's brought desert temperatures to Paris, flooding to Kansas, and other environmental catastrophes everywhere in between. Or the contamination of life's most fundamental resources—our air, food, water, soil—by known polluters. According to the Environmental Protection Agency, 40 percent of all U.S. waters are unfishable or unswimmable. In under twenty years, the World Health Organization predicts that globally, eight million people may die from air pollution.[14]

In protecting our children from injury, fearmongers also divert us from needed action. For example, we lose sleep worrying that our children might be kidnapped, molested, or struck down in a Columbine massacre. In fact, 71 percent of people responding to a recent NBC/ *Wall Street Journal* poll felt a school shooting was "likely in their community." Yet a young person in America has a one in two *million* chance of being killed in school.[15] On the other hand, in his wake-up call *The Culture of Fear,* Barry Glassner noted that five thousand children and adolescents show up in emergency rooms with work-related injuries each year, most of which could have been avoided by enforcing run-of-the-mill safety rules.[16]

All this helps explain how fear has become what French philosopher Patrick Viveret has called the "emotional plague of our planet."

It isn't hard to understand how we arrived in this sad predicament. It's not hard, but we must dig; the roots of this plague run deeper than the self-interest of government leaders in keeping us on edge, or that of corporate advertisers in fueling our insecurities.

To understand, we have to reach back in time. Way back.

Evolving eons ago within tightly knit tribes smack dab amid species bigger and fiercer than we—and with a much longer period of dependency than other species—

we learned one lesson well: On our own, we were toast. On the savanna, we didn't stand a chance. So banishment was sure death. Little wonder that not to fall in line with the modern-day equivalent of the tribe—to say "No thanks" to our fear-driven culture; to say "I have a better idea"—can seem unthinkable.

But here's the rub: To create solutions for our lives right now, and to reverse planetwide decimation of our very life-support system, requires two things of us:

- that we *do* something different than we are doing today, which is just another way of saying we must walk into the unknown;

- and that we *be* different than we are today, which by definition means that we risk separating from others.

At each of these prospects, fear is triggered, telling us to stop. The unknown is dangerous, and being different might get us booted out of the tribe, which we learned way back in our tribal days meant death. So we cave; we pull back.

Such a limited response might be a problem in any era, but what if we just happen to have been born during a brand-new stage of human evolution, one in which our inherited, pull-back responses to fear are not life-preserving but life-threatening? This is precisely the thesis of our book.

In this new stage, when the dominant corporate culture—our new hyper-tribe—is fast going global and destroying the very essentials of life, staying with the pack takes on new meaning. Eons ago it meant life; now it means death, death for our spirits, and ultimately for our planet.

Our future may depend on whether we can achieve a radical shift in our inherited view of fear, whether we can learn to see fear with new eyes. Rather than a warning that something is wrong, fear in certain circumstances can come to mean that something is just right, that we're doing precisely what is true to our deepest wisdom.

Fortunately, we human beings are not prisoners of our long-programmed responses to fear. We have also evolved a complex consciousness that allows us to look at ourselves with some objectivity. We can see how powerful are our freeze-fight-flee responses to fear, and at the same time see fear itself as a *source of energy*. The question is, how can we reroute that power to our advantage?

Consider the *Apollo 13* story. Hurtling through space after its onboard explosion, *Apollo 13* was saved because crew members had relearned their fear responses. Years of training allowed them not to freeze in crisis but to think—in fact, to nimbly *re*think all the systems and spaces. Could parts of one system be reconsidered as parts for something else? Could the lunar landing craft be used as a temporary home when all energy had to be shut down in the main craft? Sticking with the prewired plan would have meant certain death.

This little craft may be the perfect symbol of our present need to rethink and reconfigure before it is too late. Can we unplug the energy of our fear and use it to power us toward survival? Can we unplug the fear energy from the red warning light and reroute it to the green light of go? The sensation of fear is a useful bit of feedback, telling us we're in an important moment when positive action is ripe and necessary; a moment when we must evolve our understanding of our own wiring, and evolve our use of that wiring or hurtle onward toward destruction.

In our tribal roots, we feared the lion, hurricane, or drought, things over which we had little control. But for the most part, that's no longer true, as we've seen. *We're being made to fear*. Fears are being actively, intentionally whipped up. Just acknowledging how our fear gets diverted from real and addressable dangers, and is in some cases consciously stoked to keep us in line, might ignite us to break from fear's paralyzing grip.

And we can do more. We can crack one of the drivers of our fear: the myth of scarcity. The myth that there's never enough to go around keeps us on a competitive treadmill, afraid to listen to our own hearts.

We can recognize how the ethos of the dominant tribe—America's globalizing, corporate-controlled culture—creates this fear of scarcity, so intimately tied to our fear of exclusion. It tells us we'll be cast out if we don't keep pace in the endless accumulation game, after the home, the car, the right school, the hot new gadget. No matter how much stuff gets produced, human beings always want more, we're told, so there can never be enough. Some will always lose out. Like it or not, we've all been thrown into this giant game of musical chairs, a game rigged so that more and more of us end up sitting on the sidewalk.

Believing that, of course we're afraid. We're afraid in part because this scarcity-assuming idea—never enough chairs to go around—makes us perpetually aware we could end up chairless, in isolation. Moreover, it violates some really deep needs: for one, our need to be problem solvers.

If we swallow the idea that we're nothing but isolated egos in competition, any process of deliberating over a future that's good for us all—you know, that old-fashioned idea, democracy—is suspect. Watch out, the culture tells us, greedy egoists will turn any democratic process to their own selfish ends. So it's best to assume selfishness and reduce everything we possibly can to private shopping choices, right down to the essentials of life—health care, drinking water, even our genes.

How, then, can we possibly envision solutions to the local-to-global threats to our well-being, from climate change and species extinction to life-stunting hunger and spreading terrorism. Don't solutions depend on our being able to envision solutions and create a different future together? Yes, of course they do. So this shrunken view of our nature, pushed into high gear since the greed-is-good '80s, ends up robbing us of the very problem-solving tools we need. Most poignantly, this shabby caricature of our nature denies our need for genuine connection with one another. With that awareness, the words of our insightful émigré driving the taxi that day take on a different meaning.

Maybe he was only partially right, or perhaps he got it backward. Underneath our apparent fear of one another is an even deeper fear—that of *losing* one another, our fear of disconnection. The BMW owner whom our taxi driver derided for being afraid of his neighbors is probably living in fear of losing his status. What is status, anyway? It's our standing, our recognized ranking, which is the only connection some of us feel.

The dominant culture denies our need for real connection, telling us simply to compete dog-eat-dog. But wait a minute. The pleasure of cooperating for mutual benefit is embedded in our very cells! Researchers at Emory University in Atlanta used MRI scans to detect brain responses that proved exactly that. When subjects played the well-known simulation game Prisoner's Dilemma—used to explore cooperation and conflict in groups and often to prove how self-interested we are—the researchers found that the brightest signals arose when subjects were cooperating. The signals showed up "in those neighborhoods of the brain already known to respond to desserts, pictures of pretty faces, money, cocaine and any number of licit or illicit delights." These responses, said the scientists, suggest "that we're wired to cooperate with each other."[17] Cooperation, it turns out, is fun.

The scientists admitted surprise, but their findings shouldn't surprise our common sense; for how could we have survived as hunter/gatherers if we hadn't honed our capacities for cooperation?

It fits, then, that the happiest among us are those with rich friendship networks and a sense of meaning that connects to the well-being of the whole. Studies of older Americans find that whether people see their lives as having purpose is one of the best predictors of their happiness. Among those with no clearly defined purpose, seven in ten feel "unsettled about their lives; with a purpose, almost seven in ten feel satisfied."[18]

Our longing for meaning surfaced for so many Americans in the days immediately after September 11. What joy people found in offering material and emotional support to those most hurt. And countless numbers began to question whether their day-to-day work had the meaning they wanted in their lives. We humans sink, often succumbing to addiction and suicide, if we don't find that meaning. Depression, now the leading cause of disability globally, can be linked to a lack of meaning in our lives.[19] Yet in a fear-driven world that tells us simply to contract in self-protection, we often bury our need to find meaning.

Thus the root of fear, the reason many people feel trapped, even despairing, about the direction of our world, is *not* what we've assumed it was. It's not just a shaky economy or suicide bombers or ecological meltdown. It's that we've been forced to deny who we are. To discover who we are means risk—of the unknown and of separation from others. Our culture of fear tells us not to risk; yet in our hearts, many of us know that the fear of death, however great, is nothing compared to the fear that we might not have lived authentically and fully.

I, Frankie, think of a dinner I had with Dr. Mae Jemison, the first black female astronaut. She had just given an inspiring talk to a packed audience at the Radcliffe Institute. In awe of her work and her courage, I asked, "But shooting into space, weren't you afraid?"

"Not at all," she said. "In fact, I told my parents that if I died, they should never feel bad for me. I am doing what I love."

We're convinced that it's possible for each of us to live fully, to meet our twin needs for deeper meaning and genuine connection, but only as we develop a new understanding of fear. We can come to see fear as an indicator that we've arrived at an important juncture. Where we go from there will not be automatically backward, for safety may not be behind us anymore. It might mean to step forward. Sometimes fear does mean go.

A linguist has actually given a name to this need for new thinking. University of California at Berkeley professor George Lakoff defines the cultural disability "hypocognition" as the lack of a critical concept that a society needs to thrive. Examples of hypocognition and its cure fill our history.

In 1829, Quaker minister William Lloyd Garrison proclaimed in Boston's Park Street Church that slaves were men equal to all others; in so doing, he awakened the popular mind to a missing concept. The abolitionist movement, in which he took part, led to the Civil War and, more than a century later, the civil rights movement. Ultimately, the concept of the equality of all human beings opened the way to equal treatment for women, gay people, and other minorities. Today the essential equality of all human beings seems shockingly obvious. It's easy now to see how stunted we were as a society, how hamstrung, so long as such a key idea remained missing.

So now we can ask: Is the creative aspect of fear—the idea that our social fears are sometimes signals to move forward, instead of freeze, flee, or fight—possibly a missing key idea? One that now holds us back as individuals, as a society, and even endangers our survival?

The possibility of seeing fear anew, and the momentous consequences of this shift, awakened for me, Frankie, one night in Nairobi, Kenya. There with my daughter, Anna, I met the Reverend Timothy Njoya, who had done something that until that evening I believed no human being could do.[20]

As punishment for preaching a pro-democracy message even in the face of repeated threats by a dictatorial government, seven armed assailants appeared one night at his door. A slight and agile man despite all he'd been through, Reverend Njoya playfully acted out for us what happened next. As he described his fingers being sliced off, his belly slashed open, he was chuckling! . . . Me? My heart was beating wildly in my chest.

Then he told us that as he lay on the floor, certain he was dying, he began to give his treasures away to his attackers: to one, his favorite Bible; to another, his library, and so on. What! I thought, How can this be? How could anyone not respond with sheer terror and life-preserving aggression to such brutality? So I asked: "But . . . Reverend Njoya, how were you not overcome by fear?"

Sitting deep in the cushioned armchair, his sweet face framed by a stiff white priest's collar, Reverend Njoya paused for only a moment. Then he said, "Fear is an energy that comes from inside us, not outside. It's neutral. So we can channel it into fear, paranoia, or euphoria, whatever we choose." He rose out of his chair. "Imagine a lion," he said, crouching. "When a lion sees prey or predator, it senses fear first. But instead of lunging blindly in defense or in attack, it recoils." Reverend Njoya moved back, leaning on his left leg and crouching lower. "The lion pauses a moment, targets his energies. Then he springs.

"We can do the same. We can harness our would-be fears, harmonize our energies, and channel them into courage." His whole body, his whole life, seemed to tell

us, "Yes, this is possible." Reverend Njoya's response—
that of generosity in the face of brutality—so moved his
assailants that it was they who rushed him to the hospital, where doctors saved him. His ability to rechannel
the energy of his fear saved his life.

In writing this book together, the two of us have reflected many times on Reverend Njoya's story. We've
come to see that we don't have to pray for our fear to finally go away and leave us alone. Nor do we have to
reach Reverend Njoya's level of self-mastery in order to
recognize that yes, fear is *within* us, not an external
force. We can, in our own way, harness the energy of
fear and, like the lion taking aim, choose where and
what we do with it. Instead of robbing us of power, fear
can be a resource we use to create the world we want.

We live in an extraordinary era. We may be the first
in human evolution able to look at how our biology
serves us—or does not serve us—and then to choose.
We can respond in old, programmed ways, or we can
know fear simply as information and energy to use for
our own creative ends. Indeed, whether we can achieve
this radical shift in our inherited view of fear may ultimately determine our personal and common futures.

We've always imagined Reverend Njoya's attackers as seven swordsmen at his door. Now, like him, we meet our seven swordsmen. Only for us, they are our culture's dangerous ideas about fear. In the pages that follow, we ask you to open your mind to the possibility of shedding seven limiting thoughts about fear that begin each chapter and trying on for size seven new, freeing thoughts that end each chapter. Can we, like Reverend Njoya, transform our assailants into that which can save us? We have the power. Our very survival and happiness depend on whether we choose to claim it.

1

Kathryn's Cry

On Hearing Fear as a Signal

> **OLD THOUGHT**
> Fear means I'm in danger. Something's wrong.
> I must escape and seek safety.

jeff Three years ago, my sister had a baby. When they first handed Kathryn to me, she was only one day old. She was pulsing with life, yet her tiny body seemed so vulnerable. I felt too big and clumsy to be responsible for such a delicate being. How could I keep her safe?

I saw her next when she was a couple of months old, and she was crying—at least, after she spent some time with me, she was. When I would take her in my arms, her sunny face would cloud, and the crying would begin.

A baby's cry can feel like an indictment. All I could think was that if I knew what I was doing, she wouldn't be crying. I wanted to hand her off, let someone else take responsibility, let him or her make sense of it. My sister kept telling me not to take it personally, but that is exactly what I did. I watched as my sister took Kathryn in her arms, and this baby who was wailing just minutes earlier would nestle into her mother's arms silently—as though she'd never cried at all.

I asked my sister what her secret was. She just tried different things, she explained, and gradually, she began to discern what the different cries might mean. She assured me that on many days she'd listen to Kathryn's cries and not know what they meant. On those days, she just had to sit with them, offering herself as comfort in a moment of discomfort. The key was to keep trying new things, to not take it personally, and to not give up. If something doesn't work, it's not the baby's fault, or yours; you just need to try something else.

For me, this was easier said than done. When I heard Kathryn cry, I wanted to make it better in an instant. Who can bear to listen to a baby's cry? It signals helplessness, distress, unhappiness, and fear. And yet this noise, this signal, is the way babies communicate.

By the end of the weekend, I found that one thing Kathryn liked was being cradled in my arms as I danced around the room. She seemed to enjoy the thrill of the ride—protected while feeling the rhythm of life surrounding her.

On Thanksgiving morning three months after her birth, when my sister brought Kathryn downstairs, my niece was beaming. She was so present in the moment. There was nothing she needed. She was just there, enjoying what it is to greet a new day. I was reminded how simple joy can be.

When the smile faded and the cries began again, I realized I could take my sister's advice: I could now hear Kathryn's cry not as an alarm, saying something is wrong, but as a signal saying she needs something.

She might need to be rocked, fed, or put down for a nap; she might need her diaper changed. She might be bored; she might need to be carried around. Through trial and error, and some crying fits, peace comes. But Kathryn relies on us to try things out. She can't do it alone.

The year before Kathryn was born, I had begun to set aside time with myself to listen to my own fits. After spending several years working behind a desk at various nonprofit organizations, I knew something was wrong—I could hear myself crying inside. I lamented my situation with friends. I tried to forget how miserable I was by purchasing things and filling my time with activities. But no matter what music or new book I bought, it sat unread or forgotten. There I was again, with a deep feeling of unhappiness, wondering, Why am I here?

Listening to our own inner cry can feel a lot like listening to a crying baby. We don't know when it will stop; we don't know what it means. We don't know how to respond. And we often assume this not knowing means something is wrong. It's hard not to. Recently, a Boston subway public-service campaign caught my eye. It read: "Safety is knowing." If safety is knowing, doesn't that suggest that not knowing is dangerous?

Of course we're afraid of what we don't know, and most of us don't know a lot about who we are, our place in the world. So when we begin to think about what we might uniquely bring to the world, we often find ourselves facing discomfort, like the discomfort I felt listening to Kathryn's cries.

Imagine what would happen if our society treated our babies like it suggests we treat our inner calls and questions. Imagine if, when we heard babies cry, we judged ourselves to be bad parents. Imagine if we just gave up, left the baby in the house, and drove away. Imagine if we drugged our babies to keep them from crying; or imagine that those who did listen to their babies were seen as abnormal. Good parents don't have crying babies.

But babies do cry. Their cries are not value judgments. Their cries are a signal that needs to be attended to with intention.

Only as we learn to refrain from judging our not knowing can we hear our own questions. As we shift the meaning of our discomfort from something being wrong to something becoming real, new possibilities appear. In our own lives, Frankie and I have discovered that taking a moment to listen and observe the habitual urge to react, *without judgment,* is no easy task. Shifting from "fear means stop" to "fear means listen closely" requires first that we recognize fear is actually what's motivating us.

I recall my first trip nine years ago to Boston to visit my best friend. Having grown up in a small town and attended a small college in a small city, I was nervous. I didn't know what might happen. I had images of getting lost and walking into trouble.

I made sure my friend met me at the train station. My mantra was "I'll never live in a city." I equated my fear of the city with who I was.

After a few visits, my friend told me she couldn't meet me at the station.

"What? You mean I need to find my way on my own to your apartment?" I made her give me detailed directions for every step of the trip, informing me what stops on the bus were close to her house. I kept a careful eye fixed on each stop. How would I know when to get off? I didn't want to ask the driver. I was afraid of looking like I didn't know what I was doing.

Gradually, I became familiar with the city and ended up moving into the very apartment I was scared to get to by myself! Looking back, I realize that saying to myself "I am not a city person" allowed me to avoid looking with curiosity at my fear. I couldn't acknowledge it. Stubbornly repeating "I don't like cities," I stayed in the country for years, closing myself off to the many possibilities cities offer.

So was my fear real? Yes, of course it was.

For some it might take landing in Baghdad or Kabul to feel the fear of the unknown, but for me it was Boston. It's different for everyone.

As I began to acknowledge my fear, I could see it more as a marker than a verdict. It told me that I was literally in a new place. While we may try to ignore the signal, sometimes letting it lead us forward can open up entirely new worlds.

CARTWHEELS IN DRY LEAVES . . .

One early-autumn afternoon in Vermont, I stood alone under huge pines. My eyes swept from the big old barn to the sprawling white farmhouse to the rose-tinted hydrangea just past its prime— everything I'd worked so hard to make into the home and workplace of my dreams. Inside those buildings I knew what was happening. I knew the life I'd built, including my marriage, was dissolving. My body felt stiff, frozen solid with fear. My throat hurt, it was so tight. I had no idea what to do next, so I just stood there. I paused.

Suddenly, out of nowhere, a puff of new energy swept through me, like the breeze I saw tossing leaves around the yard. Before I knew it, my feet were flying into the air. I was turning cartwheels, the leaves crunching under my hands. My gut was still tight, but I had so surprised myself that I was smiling inside, too. I was literally seeing my whole life from a new vantage point: upside down. Something had shifted.

Later that day, eating an ice-cream cone in town with a friend, I felt the force of life moving

> through me—as long as I didn't dig in my heels,
> as long as I was willing just to let them fly into
> the air.   —FRANKIE

Sometimes the signal of a new direction for our lives comes from within, as in my questioning of my life's purpose. But often we're stirred by a personal tragedy or events in the world that won't let us go.

On Saturday, September 15, 2001, Stanford student Valarie Kaur Brar was watching TV at her parents' home when she learned that a Sikh man had been shot and killed in Arizona. To his disturbed assailant, the man's turban alone meant he was the enemy. Valarie is a third-generation Sikh-American; her extended family knew the victim, Balbir Singh Sodhi.

"My first instinct was to withdraw into the safety and peace of Stanford's ivory tower," she admitted. She shut herself up in her childhood bedroom with Harry Potter books, escaping to a simple world of good versus evil. But the stories only reminded her that the real world is not like that at all. "That time in retreat helped me realize that I had to take action in the world because I couldn't escape its complexity. An authentic life is the embrace of that complexity."

These critical breaks we call "moments of dissonance." They are the precious times when we suddenly become conscious of the gap between the way we're living and our heart's desire, the chasm between the way the world works and our deepest sensibilities. When we experience such moments of awareness, the question is, What do we do? Do we pull back into denial? Or do we move forward into the unknown?

Valarie chose to move forward. She hit upon the idea of bearing witness to the suffering of those who had been victims of hate crimes after September 11 and to make a documentary to help others understand their experience. "My grandfather's voice came to me to help," she said. "His words reminded me of the heart of Sikhism—*Naam Daan Isnaan,* which I understand as *In order to realize yourself, you must act.*"

Now her fears shifted, from the fear of being a member of a targeted group to the fears of a twenty-year-old who had vowed to make a film but had zero experience. Self-doubt welled up, and the performance fear quickly blotted out the fear of violence against her.

"A thousand questions started to come up. Are you really the best person for this? Aren't there other, far better qualified people to do this kind of thing with better resources? These questions are convenient, because they help you not feel guilty if you just walk away from it. Of course nobody feels that they are just the right cut.

"When it comes down to it—and this is so often left out of the calculations—it's not so much whether we're trained for it but whether it is our passion, whether it brings meaning to our individual lives. People who cross their fear ultimately take action because they realize that by doing so, their lives will be more meaningful, more complete, and will have a greater purpose. I realized that if I did not do this thing, I would be short-changing myself. I'd be blocking my own evolution."

September 11 triggered Valarie's moment of dissonance. In a very different way, this was also true for Leslie Blickenstaff, thirty, an attorney in a major Boston firm. In the summer of 2001, she'd concluded a long, all-consuming case; feeling exhausted, she'd gone to her parents' Delaware Beach retreat. She flew home on September 10, and the next day she was hard at work on the seventeenth floor of a Boston high-rise, within sight of the flight pattern of the two hijacked planes leaving Logan Airport that morning.

Understandably, Leslie's first reaction to the attack was that she just wanted to get far away, like many urbanites. She didn't want to be a target. But when work at her firm slowed a bit, and she had time to think, she asked herself, "If I died tomorrow, would I be happy about the way I'd spent my life? If I knew I were going to die soon, is this the way I would spend my time?" Her answer was no.

So she decided to try something new, using previous passions as her touchstones.

She chose to return to Chile, where she had lived during college. Being there, she thought, would help her decide whether to return to school to study Latin American literature. She chose a part of the country she hadn't seen before—Patagonia, a southern region of stunning mountains and open landscapes. Her plan was to teach English and travel in her spare time.

She asked her firm for a six-month leave, sold her condo, and flew out of Logan with four suitcases.

In Chile, she soon discovered that teaching wasn't for her. But she fell in love with the Patagonian landscape, "so empty and yet full of life and nature." She felt "there is something magical about it." Wanting to protect that magic, Leslie even convinced her Boston law firm to donate its services in helping her set up a nonprofit organization. Leslie now wants to divide her time between her practicing law, life in Boston, and her work in Chile to protect "Patagonia's mountains' calm and safety."

"I love that I've pared down my life," she says. "I like nice things, but I don't need as many material things to be happy now. What makes me happy are the people in my life and the experiences I have, not things."

When her world cracked on September 11, Leslie began to listen to herself and to acknowledge a hole in her life, but it hasn't always been easy. When she made the decision to follow her heart to Chile, her family "felt threatened by their loss of me. Some people close to me were pretty upset." And when she came back to Boston, she worried that she wouldn't follow through on all she'd learned. "When I returned to the office, it was as if I'd never left. I worried that it was all a dream."

Both Leslie and Valarie heard discomfort as a signal not to stop but to try something new. And both remind us that no step we take is "it," the final answer. The path to finding meaning and purpose in our lives is never linear. We question our path, step back, and step sideways. But we keep moving, listening to the signal pushing us along.

At three, Kathryn is now quite a talker. Her favorite activity is no longer being held in my arms as I dance; now it's having me push her in a red bucket swing. These days it's her new brother, Daniel, who is crying. Everyone is a bit more laid-back; they've been here before. I've changed, too. I hold Daniel in my arms, and I'm not scared or nervous now. I am happy. I am glad to be holding this precious baby who can again teach me to listen closely.

In my own process, the fear is still present, but I've come to see it as merely a message that the circumstances I find myself in are asking me to try something new. They are suggesting that I am in the process of growth. I know I have heard the cry before and I will hear it again.

One day when Kathryn is starting high school, or traveling abroad for the first time, or getting married, I will sit down with her and remind her what she taught me about fear when she was a baby. She will tell me that it feels so hard to stay present with the not knowing. And I will tell her she's done it all her life, and this is just another step in the journey.

When I speak with her, I will be facing my own cries yet again. It could be the cry of getting sick, of losing someone I love, of charting a new path in my professional life. So when I sit with her, I will also be speaking to myself. I've been here before, and I know that the growth came from these times of feeling the challenge and responding in new ways.

———

We often think fear tells us to contract, to seek safety, to avoid the situation, and to escape the unknown. Valarie first withdrew to the bedroom of her family home and curled up with Harry Potter. Maybe that's what we'd all like to do when faced with fear: duck for cover. But sometimes what may appear as retreat can become a moment to pause and transform fear's signal, as Valarie did.

When everything seems too big or hopeless is the perfect time to ask, What is beneath our desire for protection? Can we observe what is happening within us and not run away? Can we feel the discomfort of the baby crying, see it as a signal, and decide to try something different? When we can pause and listen to ourselves with the love we would show a struggling baby, we can begin to see that on the other side of our discomfort are new aspects of ourselves waiting to grow.

As we begin rethinking fear, it helps to remember that fear also reflects just how much we care. It was only because I love Kathryn that her crying upset me so and made me want to respond. In a sense, we can look at all our fears as measures of how important something is to us. That's easy to see in the lives of Valarie and Leslie.

Venturing outside predictable paths, we learn to expect fear. In letting go of surprise, we ease fear's sting. As we accept the unknown as frightening, we discover that as we walk into the void, we gain what we really seek: not freedom from fear but joy in discovery—about ourselves, about the world.

OLD THOUGHT	NEW THOUGHT
Fear means I'm in danger. Something's wrong. I must escape and seek safety.	Fear is pure energy. It's a signal. It might not mean stop, it could mean go!

2

Dark Matter

On Facing the Void

> **OLD THOUGHT**
> If I stop what I'm doing,
> I'll be lost, I'll never start again.

frankie In the spring of 1969, fearing I'd end up never knowing why I was here on this little planet at all, I took a deep breath and made a personal vow: I wouldn't do anything else to "save the world" until I understood how what I was doing got at the underlying causes of deepening suffering, until I could explain to myself why I was choosing one path and not another.

That meant I had to stop. I had to "drop out"—a

term that to this day makes me shudder a bit. But I did it. My husband, Marc, went off every day to his prestigious postdoc in cancer research at the university. And there I was at home, with no structure, no external identity. I didn't have children, so I couldn't call myself an at-home mom. I was just a wife in a house. A housewife—yikes! I agonized so hard over my decision that I made myself sick. I couldn't move.

At that moment I'd taken fear of my own insignificance as a signal. I wanted to believe it meant go. I was ready, even eager, to take the plunge. Like many of us, I was determined that fear would not stop me. And then it hits: We're not sure what to go *for*. We know we're on the wrong track, that's clear; but what we *could* do that's truer to ourselves is murky, or maybe we can't see it at all.

Walking into the unknown, whether a roomful of strangers, a dense forest on a cloudy night, or even a day without a plan, can be scary. Remember what ancient cartographers drew in areas beyond the then-known world? Dragons. We assume what we don't know could hurt us. Yet we realize, too, that moving toward a life we choose requires letting go of the known, letting go of our story. Perhaps it means dropping labels we've relied on to tell us who we are, or giving up structures and paychecks we cling to. Perhaps it means feeling out of place with those we care about who can't fathom what we're up to.

In any case, it means saying "I don't know." It means facing empty space and silence in a culture that equates stopping and silence with failure and indecision. We'd be foolhardy to stop even for a moment, is the lesson drummed into us, lest we lose out in the giant game of musical chairs.

There's another aspect of our speedy culture that makes such a step even more challenging. Our era may be the first in which every second gets filled. I can't ride an elevator, stand in a checkout line, or sit on a Greyhound bus without TV monitors pulling at my attention, drawing me out of myself and into what someone else is doing and what someone else wants me to think and feel and buy.

"Silence is weird" was the message of the Cingular cell-phone ad plastered on Boston buses last year. Not only are we bombarded with images drawing us outside ourselves, but we become accustomed to the feeling of constant company, even if that company is anonymous and fictitious. Silence *is* weird when we're used to the background drone of television, typically seven hours a day.[21] It's easy to feel we are never alone, never just with ourselves.

But hearing fear as a signal, really listening to it, requires that we walk into the unknown, and there we can feel very alone. (Even the word "alone" has a chill to it, doesn't it?) So as we begin, it's reassuring to understand why doing this is so difficult. It's so difficult because not only is the unknown inherently scary—we're probably hardwired for that response from our earliest days in the wilderness—but it means resisting almost minute-to-minute messages reinforcing our fear of being alone, our fear that if we stop, we'll never start again. Our fear that we'll be swallowed, rather than liberated, by our encounter with the void.

I was twenty-six when I chose to leave grad school and step off into the unknown, to admit "I don't know." One reason I was terrified is that I had to abandon all my previous coping strategies. In college, I'd tried to please my professors. More accurately, I'd hoped to trick them into not discovering I was actually the dumb southern girl that the culture of my Texas childhood had convinced me I was—cheerleader, not challenger; wife, not wave maker.

And my approach worked. I got good grades, and my professors never found me out. But my strategy hardly was a pathway for discovering my own passions; it was only what I'd grasped in desperation to avoid exposing my true self.

Then I found myself a graduate student in the School of Social Welfare at the University of California at Berkeley. I figured that since I wasn't terribly bright (naive as I was about the intellectual challenge of social work), maybe I could still contribute to the world by doing good.

But I was miserable. I knew that even if I succeeded each day in my fair-housing advocacy work in Oakland, I still wouldn't have answered my own questions about the roots of needless suffering—of poverty and hunger. I couldn't defend or explain why the path I was on made sense. But I stayed on it anyway because, well, I didn't know what else to do.

But my discomfort didn't subside. In fact, it continued to mount, so I stopped. I left school. Yes, I feared I'd never move forward again, but as the weeks passed, I did move. And soon something—novel to me—began to happen. I started listening. I started listening to myself. And when I did, I was astounded. There were actually questions coming from inside me. Questions *I* had to answer. I started wandering in bookstores and grabbing titles that explored the biggest questions of the time—poverty, politics, economics, the war in Vietnam. My questions ultimately led me from the most universal and global to the most personal of all: what we put into our bodies; that is, the food we eat.

My intuition told me that food would be my key. This hunch led me to the agricultural library, a basement catacomb where I developed a research technique I've honed over three decades. I call it "following my nose." I audited courses and attended community lectures. I read. I even learned to weave. (Well . . . I learned how to make woven belts.)

Some of you may recall that era, the late 1960s, as a time of alarming predictions that worldwide famine was around the corner. Could it be that humans had actually lost the race, overrun the earth's capacity? I had to figure this out for myself. I let one question lead to the next, and I unearthed information that would forever change my life. Not only is there enough food in the world to feed every man, woman, and child, but there is enough to make us all chubby. The "experts" were wrong.

To discover my own questions required wandering in this self-created void, allowing each question to push me to the next. The process permitted me to see what the experts had missed, not because I was smarter or had more data but because I listened to my own questions and let them take me wherever they would. I had the advantage of starting at square one, whereas those more advanced in the field had long ago leapt over it.

Part of the reason I believe it's so hard for us to face the void is that we think a void is by definition empty.

There's nothing there. Nothing there means no nourishment. No nourishment means death. Voids—hmmm, not very attractive.

Yet that's not at all how our religious traditions see it. Mohammed retreated to a cave in Mount Hiraa', in the desert hills outside Mecca, to meditate in solitude, and there he received the Koran. Jesus wandered the desert for forty days and nights before beginning his years of ministry. The Israelites wandered for forty years before finding the Promised Land, and they used that time to define their beliefs and laws. Elijah retreated to a cave to listen for divine inspiration. And Buddha wandered for six years in the forest before finally sitting one night under a tree where enlightenment came.

Our spiritual leaders found in the void their strength, focus, and insight. Their stories suggest that experiencing the void is redemptive. It is where our demons present themselves for direct negotiations with our angels, and it is that play of light and dark, good and evil, that gives shape and energy to our creativity. It is from this creativity that we crystallize our unique selves.

What if we began to see voids not as empty but as pregnant? Pregnant with infinite possibility?

Stargazing scientists have long imagined outer space as mostly empty. Now that view is passé. We know that most of what appears empty is actually full of intense energy. In fact, dark matter—what we can't see but can detect by its gravitational effects—is at least 90 percent of the universe. So the emptiness of space, like the void in front of us when we make a personal leap of faith, is merely an optical illusion.[22]

Walking into the unknown, I was stunned by what I found there. For the first time in my life, questions were coming from inside me. They led to a one-page handout. All I planned was to share my findings with a few friends, but that handout stretched into *Diet for a Small Planet*, exploding the myth that scarcity is the root of hunger. The void led not only to a book by someone who'd been given a D on her first college English paper; it ignited a lifelong journey.

But as I write of a lifelong journey, don't misunderstand. It's not, I've learned, that we can face one void and be done with it. The voids aren't a onetime affair, if we follow our curiosity. In the 1980s, peeling away layer after layer to grasp the roots of hunger, I realized that I had to let go—at least for a time—of my then-familiar role of "world hunger expert." I even had to leave the organization I'd cofounded in 1975, Food First—the Institute for Food and Development Policy. I was determined to cut beneath all the issues to what I saw as the heart of the matter: who has a voice in making the big decisions affecting all of us, the crisis of democracy itself.

Yet I didn't want to let go of my place, my home, my identity in Food First. That was just too frightening. So I tried to remake Food First to focus on my new questions, but no matter how hard I tried, others didn't see it my way—thankfully! Now, I know they were right. Three decades later, Food First is still true to its core mission, earning international acclaim for educating and energizing citizens to address the human-made roots of hunger.

A few years ago, a reporter asked me what I was most proud of having done in my life. "Actually," I said, "it's that I've kept asking the next question."

Staying with the questions, staying with my curiosity, has thrown me into the void, and from there new life has emerged over and over again.

LOVE LETTERS AT MY FEET

Last year I was asked to give a speech based on my Fear Means Go workshop. I said yes without a second thought. After all, I'd been giving the workshop for a few years. No problem; all I needed was a little time and space to think. So I took my writings and a few books to my parents' farm in central New Hampshire.

After a day visiting with my family, I sat down in front of the computer and started to write. Well, not really. I began frantically reading my previous writings, looking for something I could salvage for a speech. What exactly was it that I had to say? What were the expectations of those listening? Who was I to talk about fear, anyway? Why did I agree to this in the first place?

"Okay, Jeff," I lectured myself, "it's all a matter of discipline—just force yourself to write."

Suddenly, it dawned on me that I was writing the speech in the way many of us conduct our lives: in fear. I was trying to write about fear as if I had somehow become the expert who'd gotten beyond it. My body was tense and preoccupied; my imagined audience was there, too, breathing down my neck.

I didn't feel I had a choice.

But I did have a choice—whether we believe it or not, we always do. I could continue cursing myself and my assignment. The task would probably get done, but it would be painful and forced, and most importantly, I would ignore key pieces of the wisdom that I'd learned about fear.

This, unfortunately, is how we're taught to face most challenges. We're taught that pain is the only reliable signal that we are learning. We survive by attacking the fear with an even fiercer will to succeed, or we overwhelm it with an even stronger fear of failing. But, I thought, haven't I been telling others there is another way?

So I turned my attention to where I was. Because fear seems to cry out to us to head straight for the bright red exit sign, just sitting there can seem like defeat. But in this moment—even though I'd told myself repeatedly I couldn't afford to lose a minute—I did stop.

I looked around the room, and in this apparently empty moment, I realized what was truly on my mind: love letters sitting on the floor next to me.

They were written by two of my friends when they were first dating. After a brief time together, one of them left for a year in Greece, and the letters tell of their love across the ocean. One had bound the e-mails they'd exchanged into a book as a testament to their journey. Wondering about the possibility of publishing the letters, he sought my opinion.

I had been the first outsider to read the letters, a mixture of love, lust, loneliness, discovery, and reflection. Once started, I couldn't put them down. I was carried away to the Mediterranean, crying before I finished the first pages.

While I scolded myself for not focusing on my talk on fear, I kept thinking about my friends and their love. Finally, after trying and failing to force myself to ignore the letters, I allowed myself to finish them. My panic eased. My spirits lifted as I read of people opening and changing. And at the center of those love letters was—drumroll, please—fear!

Interspersed among the declarations of connection and future plans was fear's hand: questions about whether their love could last the separation, the specters of former loves, and the fragility of having had so little time together. These letters were showing me the interplay between love and fear—the idea that became the basis for my talk.

My friend confessed that he'd almost put them back in his backpack instead of handing them to me. Who would care about them?

How many times have we put the letters back in the backpack out of fear? Another point in my talk.

Before long, I had used these letters to say everything I wanted to say about fear. My speech was written, and soon delivered. After the talk, people came up to thank me . . . and to tell me they wanted to read the letters!

Feeling fear in the face of a challenge, we often try to squelch it so that we can perform. But what if the answers we seek come from asking, What holds the most meaning for us in this moment? We might find that what is in front of us are love letters just waiting to be read.   —JEFF

"The most successful remedy for fear has been curiosity," wrote Cambridge historian Theodore Zeldin in his mind-bending *An Intimate History of Humanity*. "It is only curiosity that knows no boundaries which can be effective against fear."[23] He went further claiming that one of science's most important discoveries about fear is that "its physical symptoms, in terms of the chemicals produced to defend the body, differ only in degree from those of curiosity." That's why those preoccupied with

an absorbing goal "behave as though they were profoundly courageous."[24]

Reading this, I realized Zeldin was talking about me
as a twenty-six-year-old. Me . . . a writer? No way. Me . . .
take on the whole world of established nutrition? No way.
Me . . . challenge the cattle industry? No way. That would
take courage I didn't have. All I had were questions I
needed to answer. That made me a writer, and because I
wrote what I had to say, yes, I did take quite a hit from
the Cattlemen's Beef Association, who tried to prove my
recipes were inedible. To the outside world, it might have
looked like courage. But whatever it was, it wasn't what I
had going in; all I had then were my questions.

Listening to our curiosity does not have to mean
quitting our job, leaving our relationship, or moving
across the country, though ultimately it might. In the beginning, it means only one thing: creating space so that
we can just listen.

As I reflected on my own experience of living alone
for the first time in a strange city, it dawned on me that
maybe the biggest reason so many of us fear being alone
to "just listen" is that our own self-talk frightens us.
Having others around can feel good because it distracts
us from this incessant inner, mostly fear-driven, chatter.
Believe it or not, one writer on fear has estimated that

we have sixty-six thousand thoughts a day, with two-thirds negative or fear-based.[25] It's tough to imagine the electrode probes on that study, but the point is clear: We scare ourselves.

In a society in which we are told our essence is consuming things, when we're battered with advertising encouraging us to be as much like the other guy as possible, little wonder we find it hard to believe that our own company could be a delight. It becomes a stretch to imagine our unique inner life as a source of pleasure, entertainment, even wonder. Interestingly, the word "alone," which now carries a sense of lack, comes from the Old English *"all ana,"* meaning "all one," suggesting completeness.

So listening to your curiosity may mean a big leap of faith. I know when I began, I thought there was nothing in there—I mean here—of much interest.

But there is another voice in the void. If we were to see the stirring inside us as an ancient cry, like Kathryn's, that merely signals us to listen, then we could understand that all we must do in the beginning is that—listen. Then curiosity becomes a direction; all it asks is that we consider another way of looking at things. Curiosity can help us engage fear differently. Instead of our being blocked by fear, curiosity allows us to inquire about where the fear is coming from. We become intrigued by its source.

In this process, we may find that curiosity is the answer to whatever questions we have. It is the voice that asks: What about this?

This kind of listening might mean wandering in a library, as I did over thirty years ago, letting one question lead me to the next, never imagining I was writing anything. With this book, I rediscovered that joy in the spacious, light-filled Boulder Public Library, as I wandered the stacks and perused the books about fear.

It might be showing up at a lecture or class or conference just because it piques your interest, though you know nothing about the topic. It might be that wandering in the park or going to a movie alone is what you're drawn to, once you drop the notion that you need another person to make it happen. It might be waking up at four A.M. to write poetry or scribble down a dream. It might be going to visit a new city or a new country, volunteering in a community-building effort, or checking out a political candidate. (Who knows, maybe it means learning to make woven belts!)

You may do something not because you've thought about whether it is the right thing to do but because you feel drawn to it; you are curious.

When I left Vermont and stepped into a huge unknown, every day my what-if-you-fall-on-your-face thinking would start up. Every day my peace came only as I found the one thing I could do *now* that absorbed me, the one thing I could do *now* that I believed was important. Jiddu Krishnamurti asked thirty years ago: "Is it possible for the mind to live completely, totally, in the present? It is only such a mind that has no fear."[26]

Yes, when you sit in the void, you sit with the fear. So keep in mind what an insightful radio interviewer in Missouri told me recently: "In today's world, it's impossible to avoid fear. It's everywhere. Since we're going to feel it, we might as well feel it because we're doing something important." You can thank fear for reminding you that you are choosing to do things differently, and that's what's important. You can congratulate yourself for attending to the urge for discovery that got you here. Just as you would listen to the baby who speaks a language you cannot yet understand, you can choose to see the dark matter inside as pregnant with possibility.

Remember, too, that a willingness to be in the void is not a onetime affair. If we listen to ourselves, we will not rest with an answer but will continue asking the next question throughout our lives. We will create new voids, opening us to new possibilities, and we will discover that the very act of showing up generates new patterns we never could have foreseen.

OLD THOUGHT	NEW THOUGHT
If I stop what I'm doing, I'll be lost, I'll never start again.	Sometimes we have to stop in order to find our path.

3

Ninety Percent of Life

On Showing Up with Fear

> **OLD THOUGHT**
> I have to figure it all out
> before I can do anything.

jeff As I was growing up, my dad always told me: *Do what you love.* Many parents say that because they know they haven't lived fully themselves, but not my dad. He never wanted to be anything other than the successful farmer he is. A few years ago, I took his words to heart: I asked myself, What do I truly want?

I did feel a little greedy. After all, shouldn't I just be grateful to have a job, *any* job? And mine was helping develop curricula to teach children about creative conflict resolution—certainly important work.

But one morning, on a beautiful spring day, I looked longingly at those passing by my office window and realized that my life was out there and not behind a desk. While I believed in what I was doing, it wasn't my work. In order to read and think about what my unique contribution to the world might be, I began taking off one day a week.

While I thought it would be a joy to spend time totally dedicated to my own interests and questions, I found fear a constant companion. I couldn't sit for five minutes; my whole body rebelled against the torture. As I sat, I began to realize why. Listening to the tape that was going through my head was exhausting. It kept telling me I was inadequate. Don't even try to find meaning, my inner voice kept insisting.

Where was all this leading me? How would I make a living? Did I really have anything unique to offer?

Eventually, I made it to the writings of Pema Chödrön, the much loved Buddhist nun and writer. Her words helped me recognize that my uncomfortable feelings were potentially positive. I grabbed hold of her phrase "the wisdom of no escape." She suggested that anyone can consciously interrupt the impulse to run from difficult challenges—an interruption that can open the door to new understanding. The power of curiosity, she said, is a resource to deflect fear's energy into fuel for exploration. I printed "curious mind" on a small piece of paper on my desk, and whenever I lost heart on my Friday adventure, I'd return to those words.

Through my own quest, I became curious about other people's experiences with less than soul-filling work, and I started questioning my friends. All were bursting with interests they wanted to pursue, the passions that called them. But I would always hear why exploring them just wouldn't be realistic. My friends were full of fear and doubt, and they hadn't even begun. They'd already translated the unknown into something dangerous. Rather than focusing on what might surprise them, they were focused on what they might lose.

How is it possible to create a more vibrant culture and livable world if most people view their potentially unique contributions as impossibilities?

This question itself became my passion. In our culture of fear, I wanted to help create a community that explicitly and consciously empowers people to follow their dreams by tapping the energy of their curiosity.

Unleashing this creativity would go a long way toward addressing the planet's predicament. At the time, my friend Emily Frank, whom I'd known since college days at Earlham College, was regularly inviting friends over to her home for what she called her "coffee-house." People would share food, then gather in the living room, though often spilling over into other rooms. The format was simple. Anyone could share anything, whether music, writing, ideas, or instructions on making a favorite dish.

Awkward silences were common at first. But as a few people began sharing, others came forward. The energy of their creativity was contagious: Guitars and a piano, short video clips, art projects, singalongs, explanations of scientific concepts, and poems filled the evenings.

I loved these gatherings. To be entertained by one another, unmediated by a TV, seemed revolutionary in our digital culture. I could feel the fun (and nervous fear) that people were experiencing at sharing themselves with others. Emily, then an aspiring therapist, was the perfect MC; she knew how to make sure we all felt supported. Everyone left dreaming up ideas for what they might offer next time.

Emily and I met frequently to talk about my interest in helping people choose meaningful work, and her interest in creative spaces. Over time these conversations evolved into an experimental organization of friends we dubbed "curious minds."

At Earlham, Emily and I had been attracted to the

Quaker belief that the divine lies within each of us, and that to receive its inspiration, we have only to listen. So we conceived of curious minds as a way to encourage people, supported by others, to listen to that often ignored inner whisper, that source of new insights about themselves and their role in the world.

About a year after I started taking my Fridays off, more than a hundred people gathered to celebrate the birth of curious minds. On a cold, crisp January evening, though snow was lightly falling outside, the energy was high inside, with musicians and poets adding a rich sense of possibility.

Soon curious minds began to hold workshops, talks, and one-on-one sessions to explore an individual's path and interests. Again and again I saw people discovering that their lives were not a random assortment of influences; they saw their curiosities and stories drawing them to create something distinctly their own.

It might be easy for most of us to relate to Stanford student Valarie Kaur Brar's initial impulse after September 11 to withdraw into the cave of her childhood bedroom. American Muslims and her own Sikh community had become targets of violence. Even after her decision to step forward and document the experiences of those threatened, her most careful planning failed to erase her fears. Instead of retreating again, she packed her car and—with her cousin Amandeep Singh Gill—pulled out of Palo Alto to begin her trek across the country.

"When we were finally on our way, out on the road, all the fears disappeared," she said. "You worry about the dangers, but once you cross that gulf and activate your agency in the world, you know you can do it from there."

Valarie and her cousin visited, listened, and filmed in homes and temples across America and India, speaking with hundreds of Sikhs, Muslims, other South Asians, Arabs, and Afghans. For her honors thesis in religious studies, she produced a film, *Targeting the Turban: Sikh Americans After September 11,* and a book for use in classrooms and communities. Her project was covered by C-SPAN.[27]

Valarie's story mirrors the lives of so many intent on making a difference and showing up—even with their self-doubt. My friend Kiaran Honderich, who lives in Cambridge, is one. Though she has a Ph.D. in economics, Kiaran, now in her mid-thirties, knew some time ago that the academic life was not for her. But she wasn't sure what was. So she accepted a friend's invitation to help with research on South Africa's small businesses. South Africa sounded interesting—until people started telling her how frightened she should be.

"I met a nun on a train in England who had worked in Africa, and she went pale at the thought of me going to South Africa alone. I became so terrified I stopped eating. But I told myself I had to do it anyway.

"It was really scary and difficult when I arrived. I remember one night lying in the bathtub and realizing I don't even feel safe here, even with bars on the windows."

The research project sent Kiaran all over South Africa. During these trips, as she interviewed small-business owners, she began to sense a strong, dark current behind many of the conversations—the largely unspoken reality of AIDS.

"One moment that sticks in my mind," she told me, "was going to a *spaza*—a tiny shop selling just a few items—in a remote area. It had no lights, and there were kids running around barefoot. The woman in charge looked dazed. She told us her husband had died the week before, and she had no idea how to run the business. She didn't even know on what terms he bought the supplies.

"It dawned on me that her husband had died of AIDS. She was left supporting nine or ten people, and she herself seemed on the verge of becoming ill. It was very hard for me to look her in the face, hear her story, and then walk away. I felt compelled to do something.

"My survival fear seemed first to be taken away just

by the pleasure I felt in getting to know people, in the music I was hearing, in the ways of life I was seeing. And then, as my concern about AIDS grew, it took over some of the space my fear had been taking up, too."

When Kiaran returned to the U.S, she created an education and direct-aid effort called Ulalo, meaning "bridge" in Swahili, under the auspices of the Center for Popular Economics in western Massachusetts. Ulalo's goal is to transform the AIDS crisis into a wake-up call about how global economics connects us all, from average Americans to rural African women.

"We are made to believe that Africans are so different from us, especially with scary and distorting media images. Many have been convinced that it must be their 'wild' behavior spreading AIDS. That it has nothing to do with us.

"We all want the same things—intimacy and commitment in relationships, for example—symbolized for many of us in a diamond ring. Ironically, in South Africa it is the mining for gold and diamonds to make our rings that makes it almost impossible for many South Africans to meet those very human needs.

"Mining takes men away from their families for long periods. Separation from loved ones, miserable pay, and life-or-death working conditions all heighten longing for connection and intimacy—the same things we want—

often leading miners to the only outlet available, the sex trade. The desperate poverty of rural women contributes, too, of course. AIDS is heavily concentrated in mining communities and the areas these miners come from.

"Whether we like it or not, we are connected to these miners and to the spread of AIDS. Now the question becomes whether we want to be ignorant of that connection or whether it can be conscious and be made into a connection that transforms both sides."

Beyond mining, the impoverishment of rural Africans, forcing men to leave their families in search of jobs, is intimately tied to policies our elected officials make in our name, here at home. For example, the U.S. spends three times more subsidizing our cotton growers—with most of it going to a handful of big operators—than on our entire foreign-aid package to Africa. These subsidies directly impoverish African farmers, because they reduce markets and prices for African cotton.[28] All together, industrial countries spend more on subsidy payments to their farmers—much of this directly undercutting African farmers—than the total gross domestic product of all sub-Saharan Africa.[29]

Most of us think of AIDS as a public-health crisis, but Kiaran's economic training allowed her to see what others couldn't: the web of interrelated economic and political roots of the epidemic, many directly tied to us.

When she made the fateful choice to accept her friend's offer to research small businesses in Africa, Kiaran never could have imagined that it would mean confronting the AIDS crisis, then work to awaken Americans to our ties to African poverty and disease. She couldn't have guessed the new use of her economics training. She just showed up with all of her fear. She showed up with observant eyes—and kept them open.

Kiaran's fears, like Valarie's, have changed. She's less worried about safety; now she wonders whether she can achieve the impact she desires in this new work.

Maybe we can never hope to leave fear behind, but by being willing to take the first leap, we put ourselves in motion. Our fears become linked to goals that really matter to us, and we take heart in witnessing our own movement.

WALKING INTO THE COLD WIND

My most recent book, *Hope's Edge,* was my children's idea. Though they were certain, my self-doubts were gigantic. After all, I'd been focused on democracy in America during the 1990s; could I reconnect with the core food-and-hunger thread of my life's work? When I was invited to MIT as a visiting scholar to write the book, my panic soared: a new city where I knew virtually no one, a new institution not exactly renowned for its warm-fuzzy ambiance.

But I made the leap, with my kids unloading the U-Haul the day before New Year's, 2000. Each morning, as I'd wrap my brown overcoat even more tightly around me, the cold wind seemed to taunt me: Just turn around, go home, give up was the message of those dark, icy days. But since I felt I didn't even have a home to crawl back to, only a lonely apartment in a strange city, I kept walking. I felt my life depended on defying the wind as I trudged among the stark buildings of the MIT campus that winter.

Day after day I would reach my tiny office, with a plain built-in desk and a window opening only to a beige brick wall; I would turn on my computer and sit, hoping, praying that something would come out of me.

Where would I even begin? Some days I could feel the fear as a tight throat; others, as a tight chest. The worst were the dry-mouth days. I would smile at faculty and students as I walked down the hall for coffee, but my insides were gripped by fear. Whenever I told friends that Anna and I were going to complete all the background research, travel to five continents for on-site research, collect and test recipes, and write the book all in one year, they shook their heads in disbelief. There are just not that many hours in a day, their eyes seemed to be saying to me.

But by early spring, I started noticing a strange phenomenon. Unexpected help just kept arriving.

On our first research trip to California, Anna and I sat in a tree-shaded outdoor café with Mollie Katzen, the pioneering whole-foods, vegetarian cookbook author and an old friend. Within minutes, without being asked, Mollie said, "I want to help. What can I do?" Expecting nothing at all in return, Mollie volunteered to oversee the selection of recipes from among those donated by leading chefs, and to oversee testing. I was dumbstruck; I knew that Mollie was pushing her own book deadline. Her generosity moved me almost to tears.

Soon after, a professor at the University of Wisconsin and a graduate student in his department of rural sociology volunteered to arrange what became dozens of interviews with farmers and others devoted to sustainable farming in the Madison area. Their assistance saved us weeks, maybe a month, of time and energy. From the foothills of the Himalayas to the Brazilian outback, others came forward as well.

Over and over it happened. Timing, people, coincidence all worked to transform the impossible into the possible.

I would laugh and quote Woody Allen, or my mangled version of his wisdom: "Ninety percent of life is just showing up!"[30] I showed up with all my fear and doubts. Then one door opened for us; then another and another.

Finally, a few months into the process, Anna looked at me and said, "Mom, I get the feeling this book wants to be born." From our experience, I came to believe that the very act of showing up—*even with one's fears*—unleashes unseen forces wanting to help. —FRANKIE

On a recent Sunday, I settled into my usual pew at Boston's Arlington Street Church, expecting another moving sermon from the minister, Kim Crawford Harvey. But someone I'd never seen before, though I had heard about him for years, rose from behind the pulpit and began to tell his story. His name is George Leger. I sat transfixed.

In 1993, George was a valued chef at a Massachusetts country club. Though he'd achieved career success, something big was missing; he felt alienated from much of the life around him. Struggling to understand why, he traced his feelings back to his junior high school years. Catholic elementary school had been a wonderful place for him: small, friendly, close, like a family. The public junior high school, however—huge, dangerous, completely alienating—was a horror. George felt that his life had somehow gotten stuck there.

So, one Sunday in May 1993, George drove the ten miles to his old junior high school in Waltham, Massachusetts, to walk around, think, and try to come to grips with what had happened there. He hoped that the visit could somehow help him resume a life interrupted.

After walking around the grounds, he got his Sunday *Boston Globe* from the car and sat against the base of the flagpole to read. The day was beautiful, and he wasn't ready to drive home. Maybe he was still waiting for something to happen. In the magazine section, he read a story about Giovanni, a young homeless boy in Guatemala who was trying to get off the street. The story caught George's eye because he had befriended several Guatemalan workers in the kitchen at the club. As he read, the story got darker and darker. Giovanni had been rounded up by the police and, after a ten- or twelve-hour torture, was killed.

The story hit George hard. He couldn't get his mind around it. He clipped it and read it again the next day, and the next. "I may have read it twenty or thirty times," he said. It so consumed his thoughts that he couldn't concentrate on his work.

He called the *Globe* reporter, Sara Terry, and she agreed to put him in touch with people in Guatemala who worked with street children. Soon George decided to visit Guatemala and volunteer with an organization helping the children.

At the time, the Guatemalan civil war was raging. Before George's first trip, he had nightmares about suddenly finding himself in grave danger, unable to speak the language or fend for himself. He woke in cold sweats. Over these months, he confronted this fear daily, determined to work through it and to make the trip.

When he arrived at the airport in Guatemala City, the prearranged representative was not there to meet him. He gathered his strength and stepped out onto the street alone. The first days were full of terror, but his fear subsided as he wandered the streets, even though he was often harassed at gunpoint by both the police and military. Every morning he felt sick to his stomach as he left his hotel, but he pushed on with a desire to learn more about the poverty and violence that had taken Giovanni.

George made two trips in 1994, finally deciding to take three months' leave from his job. At first he told very few people about his trips—two cousins and three or four friends—but then he began to share his stories with coworkers and family though he was sure they'd ridicule him. Most seemed to understand and were curious about the passion igniting George.

In July, when George arrived in Guatemala City for a three-month stint, he found that the volunteer organization he was supposed to work with had crumbled. Should he go back to Boston, or stay and work on his own? He took the weekend to walk around the city and think. Standing with a group of people in front of an appliance store, watching a soccer game televised from Boston, he realized he felt closer to the people beside him than to the Boston crowd on the screen. He decided to stay.

He walked to an inner-city park where he knew he could find and help some street kids. Partnering with someone who knew the children well, a woman who ran a food stand, he got to work. That was the modest beginning of his organization, Project Only a Child.

Flying back to the United States over a glistening Gulf of Mexico, George realized that whatever he had been looking for at his old school yard that Sunday, he had found. A deep alienation that had plagued his adult years was being exchanged for a life in tune with his heart. His tears were dissolving the wall he had built between him and the world.

In 1995 he resigned his chef position to work full-time in Guatemala. His family worried that he was throwing away a great career. His father asked him to think hard about what he was doing. George took time to rethink it all, then told his dad he was sure. That was good enough: His father supported his decision, and in time, his brothers came around, too. His friends even visited on their vacations. Twelve of them agreed to each send twenty dollars a month to finance his work.

In 1996 Guatemala's civil war ended, but not the war against children. So George stayed. He travels back to Boston from time to time, to freelance as a pastry chef and earn money for his work. Then he returns "home" to Guatemala and to his growing family of friends.

George recently e-mailed us from Guatemala:

Have I made new friends in Guatemala? Yes, many. I have become very good friends with a woman from Indiana working with children and young adults living in Guatemala City's notorious inner-city dump. I have also made friends with native Guatemalans, and of course there are the kids, who have truly enriched my life, and daily fill us with much love. In addition, we have a staff of three. A native couple works and lives in our shelter. Also we have a staff psychologist who works with our kids to help them work through all that they have suffered in their difficult lives.

On the tenth anniversary of George's program, *The Boston Globe* followed up with news of what had come from little Giovanni's death: He had not died in vain. George, untrained, lacking the language, and without much of a plan, kept showing up with his fear and learned what he needed to know along the way. Like Valarie and Kiaran, he just began, trusting that doors would open, that the force of life could be trusted. He just showed up.

In our fast-paced, outcome-driven society, we often think we need to know the answers before we can start;

we're convinced that feeling fear means we're not ready. But if we show up with our curiosity and take those first, hardest steps, things unfold in their own way, on their own schedule. As we show up, putting ourselves into new, initially uncomfortable situations, we reprogram our brain's responses.

Psychologists now acknowledge what they call "fear extinction," when people expose themselves to exactly the situations that scare them. After repeated exposure, the fear memory has to compete with the new learning that there's nothing to be afraid of. The brain relearns its fear triggers.[31] In other words, by showing up today, we change the fears we might face in the future.

Writer Jane Stern, fifty-six, took fear extinction into her own hands. After suffering a lifetime of depression and phobias about illness and death, she came up with what some might consider a counterintuitive cure: volunteering as an emergency medical technician in her Connecticut hometown. In a recent interview about her memoir, *Ambulance Girl,* Jane explained, "I thought, 'I have to do the scariest thing I think of. If I can do it, then I will be OK.' And the scariest thing for me—as a raging hypochondriac, depressive claustrophobic—was to sit in the back of a closed ambulance with a dying person, a dead person, or a crazy person. . . . It was do or die. . . . There hasn't been a day when my pager goes off that I don't get a rush of panic and think, 'I can't do this.' Then I do it and I'm OK.

"Fear is a hologram," she said. "It seems so real until you test it, and then it falls apart and there's nothing there. It's getting the nerve to test it that's hard."[32]

In any moment, we, too, can choose. We can choose to be stuck, or we can choose to hop into that ambulance. We can entertain the radical notion that what feels foreign could be our new path appearing, though it may be unrecognizable at first. We don't have to have it all figured out. We can never know exactly where we're going, and that's fine—great, in fact, because it asks our curiosity to pull us along.

OLD THOUGHT	NEW THOUGHT
I have to figure it all out before I can do anything.	We don't have to believe we can do it to do it; the very act of showing up, even with our fear, has power.

4

The Fires of Creation

On Creating with Conflict

> **OLD THOUGHT**
> If I act on what I believe, I fear conflict will break out.
> I'll be humiliated, ineffective, and rejected.

frankie In the winter of 2003, as the war against Iraq seemed all but upon us, I told myself every day that I should get myself to the office of Senator John Kerry and tell anyone who'd listen why I believed our attack would be a tragic error. Day after day went by, and something always got in the way. My hesitation tasted familiar; it was my long-standing fear of being caught off guard in a conflict, of feeling silly because I don't have all the facts at the tip of my tongue. So it was only after I hooked up with others, through MoveOn.org, that I made it to Kerry's office. With mutual support, the dozen of us were able to speak our minds confidently.

Unfortunately, the fear of conflict is pretty common. While Americans flock to action movies and stay glued to soap operas drenched with melodrama, in real life most of us abhor conflict. (How hard it is to erase those put-downs: Though it's been thirty years, I'll never forget the sting when the then-president of Tufts University dismissed my views about world hunger: "What does she know? She's just a cookbook writer.") I am convinced it's not just a bruised ego at stake; it's a primal fear of losing standing in our tribe, of being cast out into the wilderness.

Our aversion to conflict pops out in the sentiments of parents who brag about their "good kids" who "never give us problems." Or school principals whose extra praise is reserved for teachers maintaining the most obedient classrooms. Or bosses who make it clear that those who fall in line will be rewarded.

As fear spreads throughout our culture, many of us are even more tempted to run from conflict—to duck for cover. "In times of danger," wrote Rush Dozier in *Fear Itself,* "when there is no immediate avenue of escape, the primitive fear system tries to shut off any unnecessary movement, reasoning that if you stay still you might not be noticed."[33]

By not crossing anyone, we stay under the radar, or at least that's the hope of the primitive brain. Imagine the rabbit frozen motionless in the grass.

Willie Manteris, fifty-three, told me that, in effect, he'd been that rabbit most of his life. He had achieved his dream—a successful dental practice in a Pittsburgh suburb, a big home on Club House Drive, two bright children, and a wife with a prestigious job. "In my family, growing up, conflict was terrifying, destructive, and up-setting, something to be avoided at all costs," Willie told me as we sat chatting at an airport coffee shop in Porto Alegre, Brazil. "I had built my whole life by making no waves; conflict was the worst taboo, the worst fear."

But since Willie and I were both on our way home from the World Social Forum, the largest gathering any-where of citizens trying as hard as they could to make waves, something obviously had changed for Willie. Three years earlier, Willie had sold his practice to follow his heart. "The biggest fear, and the most powerful, was the hidden and invisible one: It was stepping out of the conformity and anonymity, stepping out of old roles in which I felt safe and comfortable. It meant defining the self; who I really was, who I was in the world. It meant

risking conflict." Willie did just that as he began traveling regularly to Central America with Pastors for Peace,
offering both material supplies and challenging widespread abuses of indigenous people's rights.

"One of the prices you pay for staying trapped by
that fear is that you don't learn how to express healthy
dissent. Stepping out of those shadows and voicing oneself is too scary. Politically, it put me, for most of my life,
in a role of being submissive and passive."

The consequences of staying stuck in conflict aversion, as Willie had been, are momentous. Gradually, it
has dawned on me as I've observed myself (hesitating,
for example, to get myself to Kerry's office even though
I'd long taken public stands and willingly been arrested
for causes I believe in) that fear of conflict too often
keeps good people silent, blocking us from participating
as the full-voiced citizens of a real democracy.

Even more worrisome, if we fear conflict ourselves,
we may be tempted to choose authoritarian "strong
man" leaders. In taking us to war, George W. Bush typically spoke about what "I," the president, would do, but
rarely about what we as citizens could do—reinforcing
feelings of helplessness, the sense that all we can do is
put our fate in his hands. As long as we don't feel we
have what it takes to face conflict, do we unconsciously
hope authoritarians will squash conflict for us?

Burmese Nobel Peace Laureate Aung San Suu Kyi—who, for her pro-democracy heroism, has been brutalized by a military elite, held under house arrest for six years, and is still in detention—shares this worry. She understands how a people's lack of confidence and skills in dealing with conflict can erode democratic society. "It is not power that corrupts, but fear," she wrote in *Freedom from Fear*. "Fear of losing power corrupts those who wield it and fear of the scourge of power corrupts those who are subject to it."[34]

Rethinking conflict, both as an individual and as part of a community, has become for me a key to creating the life I want and the decent society we all want.

Rethinking conflict means first recognizing that we loathe it—in part because we've been taught that conflict means failure, or at least a signal that something has gone wrong. Plus, we fear that conflict will involve humiliation. Will I start crying, I wonder, and confirm the hysterical-woman stereotype, betraying my whole gender? For men, there's the dread of not measuring up to the stereotype of masculine toughness in battle.

My family was like Willie's, teaching that conflict leads to the weakening or even the breakdown of relationships, not to their strengthening. It's no surprise, then, that terms like "conflict management" and "conflict resolution" have come to describe a whole new professional field. Despite its valuable contributions, the field's very language can carry the notion that conflict is a negative force, best wrestled into compliance (managed) or gotten rid of altogether (resolved).

Conflict also has virtues we can celebrate. It can shake us loose from narrow understandings of our interests, as we see them through the eyes of others. It exposes key information—assumptions, prejudices, values, and needs all essential to finding solutions. It can deepen our understanding of problems, often offering more options.

"Anytime we have a good rip-roaring fight, the quality of our decisions is better. Heat isn't necessarily bad," says Belle Zars, member of Save Our Cumberland Mountains, a thirty-year-old group that's taken on the mining industry in Appalachia. Its efforts passed the first Tennessee tax on coal extracted by companies, with monies going to schools and roads.

She points out that conflict can also build group or partnership confidence. Experiencing their members' differences colliding out in the open allows groups to come up with better solutions and to gain confidence in themselves as problem solvers.

While a lot of us assume we'd prefer a placid world devoid of conflict, even a moment's reflection reveals that's neither possible nor desirable—not if we value change. All change entails an encounter with a new force, often the unknown, which triggers resistance in most of us. Change also implies, minimally, that somebody thinks it's possible to improve on the status quo. No big shock, then, that somebody who helped create the status quo feels criticized.

Thus, because change—with all the growth, excitement, and surprise we love—is inevitable, conflict is, too. "To live is to have conflict," a leader in a citizens' organization from my hometown, Fort Worth, told me years ago. "If you don't have problems, you're not doing anything. This is what we're teaching our children. Friction means fire—and fire is power."

MAKE WAVES WITH YOUR LIFE

When I first tried taking the "curious minds" idea to heart, I followed my curiosity right into a middle school. Volunteering for a Boston after-school program, I was asked to teach one afternoon a week for ten weeks, helping middle-school kids produce an event that they came up with.

I charted the course; I made lesson plans. I

was meticulous. Even though I felt a little nervous as I made my way to the school that first day, I felt armed.

I would begin, I had decided, with students introducing themselves and taking Polaroids to be used for a poster capturing their interests and assets. It was all going fine until the fourth student said flatly, "No, I don't want my picture taken."

I froze. This was not in the plan.

I passed the camera to the next student, but he refused, too. Then the next. By the time we had completed the circle, I had only three photos, and I needed photographs of everyone for the next activity. What would I do? I went blank. I glared at the clock as if I could make the hands turn faster by sheer will.

The next hour, which seemed to stretch into days, is a blur. Mostly, I remember total chaos punctuated by shrieks and the occasional commands of two staff members trying to rein in the kids. Conflict was everywhere: between the kids, between the kids and staff, between my plan and the real world. I'd failed big-time.

After class, I walked back to the subway, my

nerves frayed. I was already asking myself how I could break the news to my friend who had helped set this up that I just couldn't go back.

But by the next day, the irony was already unmistakable. There I was, working for Educators for Social Responsibility, a national leader in teaching conflict resolution, and yet when I was faced with it, all I wanted to do was run in the opposite direction.

I started asking myself, What if I turned the conflict on its head? What if, every time I felt conflict with the kids, I used ESR's slogan "resolving conflict creatively" and transformed it in my mind into the unpredictable hand of creativity?

Over the next week, I talked to everyone I knew about middle-school kids. I came to realize that conflict is the way they make sense of themselves and their world; conflict is how they test boundaries. Conflict is what they live!

I started seeing new possibilities and a challenge worth showing up for. I started asking, How can I use their conflict to lead them to more successful strategies of getting things done? The kids started getting into the project, so we could talk about conflict in the context of working out solutions together.

I can easily say not one class was without creative conflict. We had decided to produce a concert, and as we planned the final production, I could feel fear creeping in and wanting to shut me down. It was in these moments that I reminded myself to keep showing up with the children where they were.

The day of the show, which the students aptly called "Make Waves with Your Life," students, relatives, and community members packed the auditorium. In the end, we pulled off the performance without a hitch, and we did it by working through conflict, not trying to erase it. —JEFF

Simply acknowledging that conflict is inevitable can help ease our fear of it. It also helps to remember that no matter how much we think we're drawn to people similar to us, to engage in relationships with others is to engage *difference*. Relating to difference is what it means to be in a relationship. It's not a side issue; it's at the heart. The attraction of opposites is no myth.

As we let go of the unthinking equation "conflict

means trouble," we might even come to see that it is in part the denial of conflict—leaving people so unprepared for it—that makes too much of today's conflict unnecessarily ugly and destructive. We have only to think of its escalation into the horror of tit-for-tat bloodshed we see in such places as the Middle East, Afghanistan, or Indonesia.

That's why one of my greatest sources of hope in the last decade has been discovering—largely through the leadership of several national citizens' movements—that the creative use of conflict is learnable. It is an art: an art we may not be born knowing, but something we can learn, just as we learn to ride a bike, play basketball, or bake bread.

For Jack Shipley, sixty-three, a part-time rancher near Grants Pass, Oregon, "fire of conflict" is more than a metaphor. It's a reality of forest management. For fifteen years, he's been living with the sparks flying as loggers, farmers, and environmentalists deliberate about the best ways to deal with forest fires and other hot-button people-and-planet issues. Being creative with the conflict that emerges when you get these disparate interests together in one room is Jack's passion. "If we don't work together, we will perish," he says.

Jack distinguishes head-against-head battling—which he says our society is addicted to—from the creative forms of conflict that produce solutions. He's working toward the latter in the Applegate Partnership, entrusted by the state with watershed protection planning for an eight-hundred-square-mile chunk of southern Oregon. "The environmentalists criticize us for talking to loggers," Jack says. "But how can we find solutions if we don't include all the people who are part of the problem?"

The essence of this shift from battling to creating with conflict is to stop blaming, he explains. In fact, members of his group wear their signature button around town. On it is one word with a slash through it. The word is "they." There is no "they" in the world of creative solutions, just different sides of "us."

But creative conflict doesn't happen by accident, as Jack would no doubt tell us. The most effective community-strengthening movements in the country are discovering several practical, obvious tactics to make conflict creative.

For one, we can train. If our fear is that we'll be tongue-tied or blow our top, we can ease that fear by learning some basic rules and by rehearsing. We can practice, just as we would any art.

———

Sally Riggs lives with her eight-year-old daughter in Des Moines. Three years ago, Sally, a medical school administrator, and her husband, Steve, fell for a credit-consolidation scam. At 18 percent, their debt engulfed them, and life quickly became hell. Sally's daughter even stopped answering the phone for fear it might not be her daddy or a playmate calling but another angry creditor. "I felt so stupid for getting into this trap," Sally says. "I felt ashamed, worthless."

Then a flyer from Iowa Citizens for Community Improvement landed in her mailbox. A force in the community for over twenty years because of its work helping family farmers avoid foreclosures, the group invited Sally and her neighbors to a meeting about launching a campaign to stop predatory lending. Somewhat reluctantly, Sally went. In a part of town that she'd always avoided for its rough reputation, next to boarded-up and run-down buildings, Sally spotted the bright green awnings of the freshly painted Iowa CCI office.

"At first I didn't like being in the company of other angry homeowners. It didn't make me feel any smarter," she says. But eventually, she started to find comfort among people struggling with the same burden. "My despair started to melt when I found out this group had fought and actually won many battles like this.

"The meetings, almost every week, started boosting my self-esteem. My oldest friends were saying, 'Welcome back, Sally,' because the 'me' that had been so beat down by stress was coming alive again."

Just three months after that first meeting, Sally found herself on the way to Chicago with a group of home-owners to meet mortgage-company executives. In earlier meetings in Des Moines, she'd always been the silent one. But rehearsing changed that.

"Before the meetings, I used to feel like I was going to be sick, I was so nervous. But the rehearsals helped. We would go to the group's office and practice making our case in their old meeting room. Joe or Tyler, staff organizers, would play the part of the executive across the table. They'd throw at us all the arguments we thought they would use. We did that as often as we could, and then, an hour before the real meeting, we would do it one last time. There weren't too many meetings when something came up that we hadn't seen coming and gotten ourselves ready for."

All this worked for Sally when her big day came in Chicago. When one financial executive seemed to dismiss her argument, Sally was hardly tongue-tied. She recalls saying: "And how would you like it if your five-year-old girl couldn't answer the phone in her own home because she was scared to?"

While she had always been petrified of the mortgage company, that changed when a busful of other victims, and supporting members of Iowa CCI, refused to leave the office of one of the worst lenders. The police, summoned by the lender, advised the cowering mortgage execs that perhaps they should solve the problems of the people in their office. They did.

Naturally, we fear power imbalances. If our adversary is someone we perceive as holding power by his or her very position, how do we balance it out? With both the power of knowledge we bring in the door and the power of our numbers—the strength we communicate and feel by having allies at our side. Sally felt that power in the office of the mortgage executives, and I felt it at Senator Kerry's office, surrounded by a dozen articulate citizens.

While Sally's husband refused to get involved and sank further into depression, her new and old friends were there for her, and she continued to fight. Within a year of her first meeting, she did the unthinkable—not only speaking out but doing so before an audience of two thousand at a national meeting. Now she's a workshop leader, passing on what she knows.

Recently, an old friend came to a meeting Sally was chairing. "I can't believe you did that," her friend said afterward. "It was just amazing." Sally's new self-confidence has also led to greater responsibilities in her job at the medical school.

Through this transformation, Sally has endured great sorrow. Her husband, Steve, had remained outside the group, and in the depths of depression, he treated Sally so badly that she moved out. Soon after, Steve took his own life, blaming the mortgage company for his despair.

Of course, Sally wouldn't have chosen the bad things that have happened, "but I wouldn't trade my new self for my old, either." All the pain made her into the person she loves being, she says, and into the mother she wants to be.

Sally's big change brings home just how important getting support and being prepared—including rehearsals—can be in transforming fear into creative power. We don't need a group to use these techniques to enable us to transform our fear of conflict. My buddy Ginny Straus, head of a peace-education center in Cambridge, and I role-play with each other when we're faced with a dicey encounter. One key is to not just play yourself. Let the other person be you in the role-play. When you hear "yourself" talking and have to respond as the other person in the conflict, you may be surprised by the new insights.

Unknown to many of us, millions of our neighbors

are finding their voices through community-building groups like Sally's. Although less visible than those providing direct social services, many of the largest organizations are faith-based and are tackling the tough root problems like school reform, environmental threats, and campaigns to replace the minimum wage with a "living wage."[35]

Moving from a fear of conflict to seeing it as our ally means gaining power through preparation and mutual support. And there's a third secret—the power of listening.

Do I sound utterly contradictory? If Sally Riggs, for example, is super-prepared for the mortgage-company executives, where does listening come in—doesn't she already know exactly what she wants to say?

Not necessarily. Being clear on what one believes can require some pretty close scripting. But in many instances, problem solving will depend heavily on listening. Jack's Applegate Partnership, for example—bringing loggers, farmers, and environmentalists together—is all about listening.

Connie Young, nearing retirement, first got involved in the Applegate Partnership a decade ago, much to the dismay of her family, who had for generations made a living from farming and logging. "I was full of fear," she says. "The environmentalists were shooting at my cousin's truck. He got his windshield blown out. So my family called me a turncoat when I went to my first Applegate meeting."

"When I stood up at that meeting and told the folks gathered I was from a long line of rednecks and proud of it, everyone laughed. A good half of the people there were environmentalists; the Forest Service was there, too. But I was able to voice my fears, and they were willing to listen. . . . It was great that somebody on the other side was willing to try to understand where I was coming from.

"And I started learning things about the other side, the people I was so afraid of. I learned from them, too. Like about the old snags, the trees we think aren't worth saving. To me they were just a fire hazard. But I found out that bats live in those trees. They are good for something! A breathing, flying animal lives in them. I started learning about the other side."

In the Applegate Partnership, with its signature NO THEY button, listening has allowed the birth of a plan for protecting the watershed that all sides are behind.

Most of us think of listening as passive and innocuous. But Herb Walters, from the mountains of North Carolina, shares Jack and Connie's view of its power. Indeed, he's made it his life's work. The organization he started, Rural Southern Voice for Peace, explores through its Listening Projects the potency of listening to empower people here and in hot spots around the world.

"It really began in the early eighties," Herb says, "when we saw that peace activists had been coming for several years to protest at the Trident nuclear submarine base at St. Mary's, Georgia. But local people weren't involved, and protesters were often seen as misguided or as troublemakers. So we trained people to go door-to-door to listen to St. Mary's residents, knowing many had jobs dependent on the Trident base.

"Listeners expected to be turned away and shunned, but instead they found people hungry to be listened to. Many opened up and shared deep fears and their concerns about nuclear weapons. Our listening established trust, and that enabled St. Mary's residents to explore their feelings openly. Some began to question the nuclear arms race itself.

"The key is treating each person, no matter how negative they seem, as part of the solution. To do this, we have to not only listen but to accept the person, even when they are expressing things we don't like—hatred or anger—or are disagreeing with our beliefs. Asking questions helps—questions that encourage the other person to explore their feelings and new possibilities. This is how we come to understand others and develop empathy. From there, trust opens the door to solutions.

"The fact that someone has cared enough to truly listen allows people to let go of their defenses and really spill their guts. It's only after they've been able to release their worst feelings and fears that they can get to their positive ideas and solutions."

Herb has seen the power of creative listening in some of the most hate-filled corners of the world. In Croatia, five peace teams that Herb helped to train took part in neighbor-to-neighbor reconciliation among Serbs, Croatians, and Muslims. Remember, these are people who had just experienced the horrors of ethnic cleansing.

These peace teams were part of a Croatian human-rights group conducting a two-year-long Listening Project in seven war-torn communities. During the project, people who had been intent on destroying each other cooperated in rebuilding sites that became peace centers. A sports club, libraries, schools, women's groups, gardens, and employment projects became places where people got to know one another and found they could work together. Listening helped to create trust, and it led to actions addressing real community needs such as food, clothing and medicine for the poor, counseling for war trauma, and housing for people displaced by the war.

"Listening is a bridge across fear and despair," Herb says, telling us how two young Serb men who one day had been part of a group chasing Muslims and shouting, "We will drink your blood," would later come up with reconciliation ideas—if they were only asked. And they were, by the Listening Project.

In my favorite story of Herb's approach, a Listening Project in Massachusetts carried out door-to-door interviews to uncover neighbors' community concerns. In one encounter, an elderly white man at first does nothing but rant and rave about "rowdy," "irresponsible" black kids who make too much noise and cause too much trouble. The problem is clearly them. The interviewers don't interrupt, don't argue. They listen and ask questions that help the man reflect and dig deeper into the issues and his own feelings. By the end of the visit, the man—after listening to himself and feeling heard—concludes that the real problem is the lack of jobs and recreational opportunities for young people.

This man got to the positive ideas after he cleared out some of the stuff that had been in his way. Perhaps it's simply that our cooperative nature, the deeper instinct, reveals itself when fear and misunderstanding are acknowledged and released.

Sally Riggs agrees that listening is powerful. "The other side of an issue isn't going to budge until they believe that they have been heard and that their position is understood and respected." Getting from "they" to "we" takes a lot of listening. You can call it conflict, but it is engagement.

Imagine if, as kids, we learned the skills that Herb, Jack, and Sally learned as adults. Today many children are. In eighty-five hundred schools, alongside arithmetic and reading, tens of thousands of young people are mastering mediation skills, with a strong emphasis on listening.[36] These kids no longer run to the teacher to solve problems or duke it out on the playground; they're finding solutions themselves. As adults, the confidence in conflict that they learned as children may, we can hope, make them less likely to turn to authoritarian leaders to do it all for them.

I confess, I grew up with no experience of creative conflict, so I operated on the unconscious assumption that if I were "nice" enough, and if I pretended conflict didn't exist, it would go away. If I don't see it, it's not there, right? Well, no. Over the decades I learned and relearned that every single time I avoided conflict, it eventually blew up, or distance grew in relationships that might otherwise have been rich.

I actually got what I most feared.

If we need a strong motivator to learn the art of creative conflict, I've found a good one the hard way: Avoiding it doesn't get us what we want. Plus, we can neither protect our own legitimate interests nor have the world we want for ourselves and our children without engaging. If we're invisible, people will bump into us. Or even roll over us.

As we acknowledge to ourselves that we are entitled to a world that treats us with respect—whether it's by the president of the United States or a boss or a friend—and act artfully with the conflict that can ensue, we become more human. Or at least human as philosopher Karl Jaspers understood it. "Being human," he has said, "is not being driven but deciding what one is going to be." I like that definition. Or, as Viktor Frankl has written, "being human is being responsible . . . responsible for one's own existence."[37] As we learn to engage with conflict, we become more responsible, feeling the dignity that is our birthright.

With my diagnosis of breast cancer this spring, I got the chance to go beyond my habitual conflict-avoider mode to become more responsible. I discovered I could tell one surgeon who made me wait two weeks (using her vacation as an excuse) to learn I had a worrisome biopsy that I'd lost confidence in her care. I also managed to tell the same thing to my next surgeon, who hadn't even bothered to look at my records and belittled me on our first encounter.

Sure, it felt uncomfortable. I feared the hospital would label me a troublemaker. But the rewards—ah! A nurse confided that she was glad I'd registered my dissatisfaction; the doctors really needed to hear it. Maybe I've made things a bit better for the next patient. Plus, I ended up with a dream team, physicians who are off the charts in both their caring and their competency.

Think of all the energy we spend trying to skirt or keep the lid on conflict. Think back to a moment when you stopped trying to avoid it and engaged with it instead. Recall the sigh of relief inside and the energy released—fear fading as self-respect grew stronger. Now imagine the freedom as you trust yourself to see and to meet conflict as opportunity.

OLD THOUGHT	NEW THOUGHT
If I act on what I believe, I fear conflict will break out. I'll be humiliated, ineffective, and rejected.	Conflict means engagement. Something real is in motion. It's an opening, not a closing.

5

The Dragon's Mouth

On Enemies as Teachers

OLD THOUGHT

Our greatest fears are our worst enemies;
they drag us down and hold us back.

jeff A year ago I had a dream: A monster is chasing
me. It's hunting me down. I run as fast as I
can, not knowing if the monster is around the next corner. I continue running but begin to tire. I wake up with
sweat pouring off me.

———

Despite growing up in the rough-and-tumble of farm life, I preferred playing make-believe, writing poems, and spending time with girls. On the bus to and from school, in gym, in between classes, and during study hall, I faced endless threats of physical violence, spitballs, jeers: "You girl, queer, sissy, fag."

I said nothing about my daily trials to my parents. I tried to hide my suffering from them, but I wasn't measuring up at home, either. My mother lamented that she didn't have a son interested in farming. "Your poor father," she would say.

On the yearbook committee in junior high school, our "job" was to predict our classmates' future careers. Secretly, I dreamed of being governor of New Hampshire (I could never be accused of thinking small), but when the committee got to me, one of my classmates blurted out, "Hairdresser for models."

Shocked and embarrassed, I protested, explaining that I was interested in politics. But no one listened. Hairdresser was my future. In spite of my school success with following the rules, I had been stereotyped and labeled by mannerisms I thought I'd covered up.

Instead of letting my pain teach me to let go of others' opinions, my fear of future embarrassment was so overwhelming that I resolved to do whatever it took to avoid it. I told myself to get with the program. During high school, I did some of what I wanted and a lot of what I thought I should do: joined student government, made National Honor Society, went to the prom. I was active, and I was unhappy.

I remember a voice inside telling me, "If you let yourself be gay, you will grow up to be unhappy." I vowed I would not let this happen. During the one conversation about gay rights that I remember from school, I said it was fine for gays to do whatever they wanted as long as they weren't near me. Gay was something I refused to be.

But this denial finally stopped working; it was too uncomfortable. When I moved to Boston to attend grad school, afraid I would never experience the life I am on earth to live, I resolved that I would create an honest life and started to date men. I quickly realized how limited my view of gay culture had been. Gay men are like the larger society, with as many people breaking the stereotypes as following them.

When my parents decided to visit me for the first time in Boston, I was thrown against my deepest fear. I was still afraid to tell my parents who I was. But how could I hide it? I had a boyfriend and bookcases stacked with such not so hard to interpret titles as *We Are Everywhere: A Historical Sourcebook of Gay and Lesbian Politics* and *Novel Gazing: Queer Readings in Fiction.*

I couldn't imagine putting on a show for my parents,

pretending nothing had changed. So I wrote them a letter, coming out to them. The day after I mailed it, my mom called. I could tell from her voice that she hadn't received it.

I tried to make small talk, but all I could think about was that everything had changed. I knew I had already been honest with her, even if she wouldn't read it until the next day. At last I blurted out the words, "I have something to tell you."

To me, these words have always meant something deadly serious. They signal a disruption, a conflict. I was so afraid. I knew my mom had no reference point for what I was about to say. There were no openly gay people in my community or in my extended family. No aunt or uncle to compare myself with, and this was before *Will & Grace*.

I leaped into the void. "Mom, I am gay. I'm sorry."

I had never experienced such fear. I had just told my mother something I had denied for years, even to myself. I said I wished I didn't have to hurt her and that I was seeing someone and living an open life in my community.

I began to cry. I could only imagine the images flooding her head: of happy weddings and grandchildren against miserable and unhealthy gay men. There I was, confronting my own deepest fear of rejection from someone I trusted, and knowing that I was also probably provoking fear in someone I loved.

I honestly don't remember the conversation we had that evening, only its end. My father had just come in from milking the cows. "Do you want to tell your father?" my mother asked.

No, I said, unable to hold back more tears, and hung up. Telling my father would have been too much.

Crying and upset that evening, I sat wishing it would all go away. But I knew there was no turning back, and the knowledge that a new era of my life had begun gave me strength even in my nervous fear. I had faced the most elemental fear—that I would not be loved for who I was—and I was still breathing. I did not know what it would mean, but I knew from that moment, life would be different.

It was not easy. While my mother sought to understand her new identity as a mother of a gay son, my father and I didn't discuss it. The stereotypes my parents had grown up with, and the prejudices in their community, made it all the harder.

It might have turned out differently. There are too many stories of young people being thrown out of their homes for being honest about who they are. There are too many stories of awkward family gatherings and parents who do everything to avoid relating to their child's sexuality. There are too many stories of gay youths, doubting they have a place in the world, taking their own lives.

I hope that even if my parents had reacted harshly, I still would have gained strength just by speaking truthfully about who I am.

MY MOUNT AUBURN SPA

I guess it wouldn't be an exaggeration to say that breast cancer is every woman's worst nightmare, next to losing a child, that is. Oh, we're sure it could never happen to us. We think that way especially if we believe we're doing it all right, faithfully reducing all our risk factors by eating healthfully, exercising, not smoking, keeping our weight down. Yes! We're safe. It can't happen.

That was me. That was me until one day in mid-February, when I was having coffee in a café with Anna. My cell phone rang; it was my surgeon. "You know that report from the GP that your biopsy was great? Well, it's not. You have precancerous cells. We'll have to go in again."

Okay, that's not so bad, I thought . . . until two

months and two "procedures" later, and another call from another surgeon: "You have a rare breast carcinoma," she said. "It's not aggressive, and we removed it, but you'll need six weeks of radiation."

I, I, *I* have *cancer*? (I can write the word now, but at the time I couldn't even say it.)

I was facing shock, six weeks of radiation, and a book deadline, all in the same summer. Plus, the week I got the big news, my sweetheart had left town on a long-term assignment of his dreams, something I ardently wanted for him, but that made it even harder to confess how much I'd miss his support. I joked with friends that the universe was simply being helpful: After all, I'd announced I was writing a book about fear. I could always use more material, right?

I laughed, but I also cried, a lot. It wasn't the disease so much, or even fear of dying. The unknown was most scary. Even though my friends stepped in and my kids came to visit, it was my devious mind telling me I was walking alone into the unknown that brought up tears.

During my first two days of radiation, the tears kept coming. "How are you feeling?" asked the doctor. "Weary, teary, and bleary" was my summary. But within a few more days, something started to change.

Before the radiation, I'd decided, with my friends' help, to explore all sorts of get-healthy initiatives. I consulted a nutritionist who specialized in fighting cancer. Every day I ate my seaweed and my cruciferous vegetables (love that coleslaw!). I went for acupuncture and saw two Chinese herbalists. I started getting Reiki treatments and listened to a relaxation tape at least once a day. I committed to doing yoga each morning. I was focusing on health with new intention, and I was actually following through.

Whenever I had a choice between pushing hard on my projects or being kind to myself, I chose the later. (Well, most of the time.) I even picked midday for the daily radiation, instead of pressuring myself to get it out of the way early in the morning.

Sometime in the second week, it dawned on me that I was doing what I had never given myself time to do: really focus on my health, my peace of mind. It was as if I'd just checked in to an expensive spa, right down to the hefty bill. (My insurance isn't great.) So what if I just called it that? I decided to reframe my treatment as my own special self-care prize. I told my friends I'd joined the "Mount Auburn Spa," naming it after the hospital. I even started looking forward to my time at the clinic. If I had to wait, I was able to finish the entire newspaper, a rare luxury. After each treatment, I'd take time for lunch. Before, I was munching in front of the computer.

In claiming this time for myself, I've also found my fear of the unknown dissipating. I've allowed myself time to reconnect with my friends, my children—I feel more supported than ever.

And the cancer has given me renewed energy in my life's work. It is my personal reminder that we're on a planetary death march. Of the eighty-five thousand synthetic chemicals we've put into the environment, many are known to cause cancer.[38] By some estimates, two-thirds of Americans live in areas where toxic chemicals pose an elevated cancer risk.[39] So it doesn't surprise me to learn that known risk factors like family history can't explain most breast cancers.[40]

> Today I'm one-third of the way through. Yes, I still fear my energy will flag before our book is finished, but mainly, I'm just grateful—for my loved ones, for this reminder that the work we do to improve the planet is really a matter of life and death. And I'm grateful for being forced to listen to my own advice (never a bad idea in a pinch!): that reframing my experience could turn something frightful into something life-serving.
>
> —FRANKIE

It's often possible to look back after a frightening experience and see what we've gained. That's a first step. We discover that the moments we've most feared have brought us closer to who we really are. The ultimate power shift, however, is recognizing this truth *as* we are experiencing the challenge; to face an enemy or obstacle and *in that moment* know it as our teacher.

I would never say that my being misunderstood and harassed as a child was good, but these negative voices forced me to grapple at an early age with who I am. The confusion I experienced growing up provides a contrast to the clarity I feel today. I feel fortunate to be aware of that contrast, to know what it's like to live in a self-imposed prison and what it's like to live in freedom.

Before coming out, I lived with fear moment to moment, always looking at the world as a threat. Now I can barely remember that burden. The experience of being honest about one aspect of myself gave me the courage to look at other areas. I could see that I was beginning to choose, not merely react. I was discovering the essence of freedom.

In many ways, all of us, not just gay people, are in a process of coming out to others about who we truly are. Early in life, we learn to follow the promptings of peers and to please others. But this isn't enough. We all want to experience parts of ourselves that might not please those near us. The fear of revealing ourselves is often a signal that we are on to something big.

I know that my personal challenges are relatively modest ones, as I was reminded when I first met Arn Chorn-Pond. Before I ever heard his voice, I heard Arn's soul in his flute playing. He'd performed at a gathering that brought together people from the world over who shared one thing: the experience of unspeakable terror.

As I learned about what Arn had been through, his

spirit and love for music seemed even more impressive. Arn was a child in the 1970s, when his homeland, Cambodia, was torn apart. In a campaign of genocide carried out by the Pol Pot regime, Arn's entire family—musicians and actors—died of starvation. All told, nearly two million Cambodians lost their lives, but Arn survived—only because, as he later told me, the Khmer Rouge soldiers needed a flute player, and he outperformed other children. Arn was forced to play his flute while witnessing the slaughter of hundreds of his compatriots, including babies. On the threat of death, he was even made to assist the executioners by stripping victims before they were killed with makeshift pickaxes. Drafted to fight the Vietnamese as a teenager, he escaped to the jungle, where he lived by following monkeys to their food sources. Eventually, he stumbled into a refugee camp in Thailand, where an American aid worker found him, brought him to the United States, and later adopted him.

"From the time I was eight, I lived mostly in fear," Arn told me. "At first it was that I would be separated from my family. And then this came true. I lost all my family. So then the fear was for my own life. Under the Khmer Rouge, life might be taken away any minute. The fear was constant."

Arn, now thirty-eight, divides his time between Lowell, Massachusetts, where he works with Cambodian gang members, and his birth home. In Cambodia, he's helping to retrieve the country's traditional music and the performing arts that Pol Pot tried to eradicate. Through a program Arn initiated, Cambodia's master musicians are now passing their art on to youth. Music, which literally saved his life as a child, is now giving him new life.

When I told Arn in Cambodia that I was calling from New Hampshire, he laughed. He'd grown up in this state.

"In America, I constantly wanted to kill myself. I had lost all my family, and I had been through terrible things. I was haunted by nightmares. But then I thought, If I kill myself today after going through these things, is it better for the world? When I began to speak about my experience and to travel, I realized that the world is round and that I was not the only one who went through this experience. Speaking with Israelis, Palestinians, South Africans, Tibetans, Rwandans, and people in Northern Ireland, I realized that we are all fighting the same fight.

"Before I was forced to live in fear, and now I choose. Now I go out on the streets. What do I have to fear for? I'm doing this for me. People say, 'Stop taking so many risks, Arn, we want you to live longer.' People are so afraid of dying. But we *are* all going to die. If I die doing what I believe, so what?"

I was struck by these words. Most of us will admit that we fear death, when maybe what we fear is dying without knowing why we're here; dying without living first.

Arn now works in Lowell's roughest neighborhoods, those controlled by drug lords. "I have no choice but to trust people," he told me. "I do the opposite of fear. That just opens the door to every opportunity. In the end, it is just a vibration coming out of you. If you go to someone with fear and mistrust, you will get it back. People respect me for who I am, not the money I have, not the car I drive or the clothes I wear. I have nothing to convince them. I have nothing to buy them.

"In the fear-and-greed environment, we forget being a human being. It's the natural, the simplest, things we can do. Hugging each other, smiling at each other. It's what we all want, but we forget about it. We look for complications, but the simplest things we do not do."

By the end of our conversation, even over the tens of thousands of miles separating us, I felt the vibration of love he was talking about. The pain and guilt are still with him, he says. So why haven't they destroyed him? The strength of his voice and his energetic drive reflect purpose and meaning. Even though our situations are incomparable, Arn teaches me that as we feel ourselves useful to others, our own fear diminishes. Psychologist Viktor Frankl noted half a century ago that his patients who became involved in serving something beyond themselves recovered from difficulty more easily.[41]

In part, it has to do with our power to decide what any experience will mean to us. Frankl stated, "Man is *not* fully conditioned and determined but rather determines himself whether he gives in to conditions or stands up to them. In other words, man is ultimately self-determining. Man does not simply exist but always decides what his existence will be, what he will become in the next moment."[42]

In my dream, though I'm half awake and sweating, I decide I don't want to run anymore. I seek out the monster. I stare at it from across the room. It's a large reptilelike creature with scales and a huge mouth. I wonder what might happen if I embraced this monster instead of fleeing. The energy I have spent avoiding it is now my motivation for confronting it.

I have no idea what might happen. But from where I am standing, I take off running and fly right into the mouth of the monster.

Instantly, everything shifts. I am now floating with an intense feeling of love. There is no dream. No monster and no me. There is only a feeling of overwhelming love and connection.

After this moment, I am then outside the monster

again. I look at where it had stood. There, on a pedestal in front of me, is a stone statue of a serpent eating itself.

This dream has become my touchstone, reminding me that we need not run from our monsters. Maybe I'm learning the meaning Rilke intended in the passage that opens our book: "Perhaps everything that frightens us is, in its deepest essence, something helpless that wants our love."

Even after running for so long, I didn't consider turning around. Yet when I did, I could recognize my own power to find the meaning of its presence. In seeking it out and confronting it, even embracing it, I realized that its power to control me was power I had given it.

Late one afternoon last summer, while waiting on customers at my parents' farm stand, I looked up to see that the man standing in front of me was one of the meanest, most terrifying of my childhood bullies. The kid whose threats so worried counselors on a Boy Scout camping trip that they made me sleep in their tent for protection. I recognized the boy in the eyes of this grown-up man; I wondered if he recognized me.

My first reaction was to constrict in fear. Intervening years could not stop it. However, as I helped him with the vegetables, I realized I was no longer that little boy, that there was nothing he could say or do that would make me afraid. As he walked away, I felt compassion for this man and was thankful for my own unique path. Seeing him again was a gift to help me realize how far I'd come.

OLD THOUGHT	NEW THOUGHT
Our greatest fears are our worst enemies; they drag us down and hold us back.	Our worst fears can be our greatest teachers.

6

The Kayakers' Cove

On Choosing Our Tribe

> **OLD THOUGHT**
> If I'm really myself, I'll be excluded.
> If I break connection, I'll be alone forever.

frankie Every spring, enormous lilac bushes bloomed just outside the office windows of our gorgeous forty-five-acre compound in rural Vermont. Entering down a long, pine-lined drive, you could find me in a rambling white farmhouse—the oldest building anywhere around—bustling with as many as twenty staff and volunteers. We were promoting what I call "living democracy," a vision of democracy as a way of living that can move us beyond the indecency of hunger and poverty amid plenty.

It certainly looked like a community, and one I'd spent most of a decade building: making a cozy home out of a ramshackle barn, painting lawn chairs for outdoor staff meetings, planting my first morning glories.

Lively interchange, collaborative projects—these were what I relished, along with staff picnics replete with badminton and horseshoes. They were rich years, so I tried to bury any conflict as well as my gut sense that, while the work was important, I was not fully using my gifts. Much, maybe most, of my time was spent raising money and worrying about budgets and staffing. I was afraid, though, that if I let up on those fronts, the organization would collapse and I would end up bereft of community. I thrived on those staff meetings around the old plank table.

When I felt called within to take an unpopular stand and many turned against me, I froze. Fear of loss paralyzed me. My body felt the weight of my fear. Feeling ill, I visited the Quaker healer John Calvi, who has worked with survivors of trauma much more dire than anything I was experiencing. As we sat in his rustic farmhouse in Putney, a nearby village, John looked me straight in the eyes. "Frankie," he said, "it may be time for you to go out into thin air."

I felt a cold chill seize my heart, because I knew he was right. But, I wondered, could I even *breathe* in thin air?

Looking back, I see that the fear of breaking with community is deeply rooted in the human psyche, more deeply than I'd ever imagined.

This might be a bit of a stretch, but try it: Imagine it's twenty thousand years ago. There we are together—you, me, our families—just a handful of us compared to today's six billion plus. We live day to day by trusting one another to share the spoils of the hunt and to pass around the fruits of our day's gathering. We know we couldn't survive without one another. Charles Darwin understood this, ironically—given that most of us associate him with the decidedly anticooperative notion of "survival of the fittest." But Darwin appreciated that primal people must have judged what was good or bad solely on how it affected the welfare of the tribe.[43] That's how well they grasped the importance of the tribe to survival. Banishment was certain death.

Consider also that, compared to other species, our young are dependent much longer on their parents' nurturing and protection. These two features, an early evolutionary experience of being utterly tribe-dependent and our longer caretaker dependency, leave a mark—a deep mark on our perception of where safety lies. Scientists tell us that we experience the pain of being rejected as very similar to actual physical pain.[44] We're programmed to feel that our survival depends on inclusion. Therein lies a huge opening for fear to walk in.

So intense is our fear of expulsion that some of us find the risk of immediate death preferable. As the U.S. geared up for the war in Iraq, I heard a pilot interviewed on the radio. The interviewer assumed that the pilot's greatest fear would be having his plane blasted out of the sky. No, he said, his worst fear was "f—ing up." It was the thought of disgrace that haunted him—a loss of standing in his squadron, his tribe. In *On Killing*, Lieutenant Colonel David Grossman underscored this truth about soldiers: The terrible, life-shattering stress of war that soldiers experience is less the fear of dying than the fear of being perceived as letting your buddies down.[45]

This deeply cut fear of expulsion from the tribe once made perfect sense. But what happens when we carry that baggage into today's world, a world in which our whole tribe may be about to paddle our canoes right over four-hundred-foot-high Victoria Falls? What happens if *you* can see the high falls looming in the catastrophic consequences of global warming and deepening global poverty, but most of the tribe can't, or they remain stubbornly in denial? Do you try to turn the canoe around or leap out and scramble to shore? Do you call others to follow?

Maybe that's just where we are today; maybe those *are* our choices. Today an anticommunity, corporate-driven culture is going global. It's eroding life's essentials, from clean air and safe water to topsoil and diverse species. It's fostering anonymous, competitive, fear-filled ways of relating to one another that deny the human need for community. While staying with the pack always meant salvation to our species, now a willingness to break with the pack may be our real hope. What a time to be alive!

This is the core challenge laid out in our opening chapter. We know that our own personal happiness, our need for meaning, depends on developing our unique gifts. But for many of us, the very awareness of our uniqueness brings with it an awareness of difference—and therefore the fear of disconnection. From there, it's a quick step to the old thought beginning this chapter: "If I break connection, I'll be alone forever."

But human beings can rise to this challenge. We can acknowledge our deep need for one another and still be able to break connection when it doesn't serve us.

Certainly, it's silly to deny our need for connection. In fact, the whole notion of the independent, creative trailblazer—alone in defying convention—is a myth.

Most of those we've long seen as lone geniuses—take Sigmund Freud, for example—were supported by a circle of intimates and collaborators.[46] Or consider Michelangelo. We can almost see him laboring alone on high scaffolding as he painted the ceiling of the Sistine Chapel. Actually, thirteen people helped out. Michelangelo was an entrepreneur who collaboratively made art bearing his name. Painters Georges Braque and Pablo Picasso were intensely collaborative, an association that gave birth to the Cubist school of modern art. For years, they talked constantly, seeing each other almost every day. Later, Braque compared their creative interdependence to "two mountaineers roped together."[47]

The trick is not to deny our need for connection but to believe we can become conscious choosers of it. Not snooty, not judgmental—just choosers. We can choose to bring into our lives those who reinforce us on our truer paths. On that canoe ride to disaster, we can find other doubters before it's too late; we can paddle in a safer direction, or at least jump ship together.

Recent findings in neuroscience relate to both this challenge and its solution. They tell us what our life experience has probably already shown. The depth of our interdependence is greater than we'd imagined: We literally experience and therefore cocreate one another, moment to moment.

Just a few years ago, Italian neuroscientist Giacomo Rizzolatti was studying the brain activity of monkeys, particularly in the part of the brain's frontal lobe associated with specific actions, such as reaching or eating. In response to different actions, Rizzolatti saw specific neurons firing. But then he noticed something he hadn't expected: The same neurons fired when the monkey was simply watching another monkey perform the action.

"Monkey see, monkey do" now takes on a whole new meaning. Assuming we humans are wired like our close relatives, simultaneously with any person we are observing, our own brain is experiencing at least something of what that person is experiencing.

Rizzolatti called these copycat neurons "mirror neurons." To me, their implications are staggering. We do walk in one another's shoes, whether we want to or not. Our inner experience is in part created by the people we observe. Cultural historian and futurist Steven Johnson would go even further. In *Emergence,* he wrote, "It's conceivable that mirror neurons exist for more subtle, introspective mental states—such as desire or rage or tedium—and that those neurons fire when we detect signs of those states in others."[48]

When Anna and I were writing *Hope's Edge,* we said

that our "imprintability itself is a source of hope; we 'become' each other in some mysterious way, and it happens without our even knowing." One of our editors, a dear and very smart friend, challenged us: "What does that mean—we 'become' each other?" Well, at the time we couldn't really defend the sentence, but we clung to it anyway. We didn't imagine that there were experiments going on in Italy right then that would prove how linked our experiences truly are!

To us, these new findings mean that we're continually in a process of creating ourselves and, most reassuring, that we can take charge. We can do a lot more than make New Year's resolutions or even consult a shrink. Since we shape ourselves in part by what we observe, we can evolve who we are—including creating lives of greater richness and impact—by changing who and what we expose ourselves to.

However, in order to begin this process of more conscious choosing, sometimes we must risk it all. We must risk disconnection. We must risk expulsion. We have to walk right into that primal fear, which is just what I experienced not many years ago in Vermont.

Soon after John Calvi suggested that it might be time for me to step out into thin air, my community did dissolve. All my worst fears came true; I'd never felt so alone, so frightened. But something else happened, too.

I remember the first call. "Hi, I'm Anne Black. Remember me? It seems like you're going through a tough time. Maybe you could use a friend. Can we meet for lunch?" That call led to many lunches together and to toasty hours in front of Anne's fireplace on bitter Vermont winter nights, reading aloud to each other. It even led to our being able to cry together through the death of loved ones.

Not long after Anne's call, others came. "You need support. I know two people you'll love," my acquaintance Mary Ann Carlson said. She and I had met decades ago, during my days as a young mother in Hastings-on-Hudson, New York, but I'd never bothered to travel the hour's distance between us in Vermont to develop the friendship.

"You've got to meet Sylvie Blanchet and Andrea Diehl," Mary Ann told me. Within months, a four-way friendship took root, and it's carried us into our deepest fears of the unknown together.

One summer we strapped four kayaks on top of a car and headed east to a quiet cove on Penobscot Bay, Maine. Most of us were new to sea kayaking, but we ventured out from our cove together, learning to dodge lobster boats as we paddled from one tiny island to the next. Soon we anointed ourselves the "Kay-yakers" as we gabbed and paddled along the Maine coastline.

In a faded Victorian with a broad porch facing the water, we danced and sang as we cooked together each evening. Its Tuscan-yellow kitchen became our favorite hangout; where at week's end, was hard evidence of our shared pleasures: five empty wine bottles and almost that many olive-oil bottles. One afternoon, in a clearing in the nearby woods, the Kay-yakers created a ritual to mark the beginning of my journey to write *Hope's Edge*. Since then, we've worked for and with one another in various capacities.

Just when I believed I'd lost community, I discovered that I was only beginning to know it. The end of my community in Vermont propelled me into these new friendships, a new life in Cambridge, and the writing of *Hope's Edge*. That project reconnected me with dear friends in the European food-democracy movement with whom I'd lost touch twenty years ago.

So I felt a click of self-recognition when Willie Manteris shared his own experience. "After I sold my dentist practice to follow my heart, I found myself pulling away from old relationships," he said. "And what I have found instead are different types of relationships. They are extremely meaningful, deep. I find this even with people I am meeting for only a short time. And they might not even speak the same language as I do. Maybe the word is 'connection.' I feel confident the other person understands my heart completely. These types of connections are possible once this change, of being truer to yourself, occurs."

In my case, the end of the old life also made way for new depth in my relationship with my kids—traveling the world and collaborating with my daughter, and anticipating a writing venture with my son. Experiencing the loss of connection I most feared actually led to rewards of connection so rich I never could have dreamed them up.

In this adventure of choosing our tribe in order to become truer to ourselves, the art is not just in selecting associates; it's not only a question of whom we marry or choose as friends, not just where we work. The stimulation of our mirror neurons—no doubt linked to our mimicking capacity—likely goes on as well with the people and activities we see on television or in the movies, or hear on the radio.

Changing ourselves means carefully choosing our mental diet. Having written *Diet for a Small Planet* in my twenties, I've long been associated with a call to choose thoughtfully what we put into our mouths. Decades later, I've begun to see that maybe even more critical is what we put into our minds, in part because these choices ultimately determine what we put into our mouths. In our increasingly fear-driven world, maybe we need to consciously choose a "hope diet."

Over half of all Americans say that television is their primary news source, but a hope diet might mean, for example, cutting out sensationalist television news. Its negativity is immobilizing; it is anti-hope. We can instead choose magazines, online news, radio, and television programs that inform without fearmongering; that show possibility. (Remember, C-SPAN isn't just arcane government-committee hearings; it's news without the hype.) Most importantly, we can expose ourselves to stories of people who are creating hope through action. They allow us to believe ourselves capable. Jeff and I include our own hope-news picks at the end of the book. You no doubt have ideas of your own.

That we humans take our cues from one another is exactly why Anna and I wrote *Hope's Edge* the way we did, as stories of real people creatively acting against high odds. We hoped our readers would begin to carry these people within themselves, as Anna and I do.

Wangari Maathai is one. In Kenya in 1977, she planted seven trees on Earth Day to highlight the environmental crisis, especially the destruction of her

country's forests. Faced with personal, even physical attacks for her pro-environment, pro-democracy work, and laughed at by government foresters, she walked on. The foresters insisted that unschooled village women couldn't plant the trees that deforested Kenya so desperately needed. But from Wangari's first simple act and her ongoing courage has grown a movement of village women that eventually created six thousand tree nurseries. Two decades later, they've planted twenty *million* trees throughout Kenya. Last year, when President Daniel Arap Moi was defeated and Wangari was elected to the new parliament, women danced for joy in the streets of Nairobi.

Wangari's photo hangs just over my right shoulder. Yes, I admit, I don't feel I could ever be as courageous as she, but carrying her with me helps me believe in human possibility, even my own—so that I walk taller with my fears.

We've all read about people who seem to be more courageous than we could imagine ourselves to be. Can we learn to muzzle ourselves before we say: "That's not me; they are different"? Maybe they are just doing what they love, like the astronaut I met; maybe they just trained hard, like Sally Riggs. In any case, can we teach ourselves instead to respond: "Maybe *I* can do that,

maybe I can be like that"? It might be easier once we understand that even by observing them—science assures us—we make them a part of us, their courage and all.

If we're willing to risk loss, if we stand up, our actions declare that we have a vision of something the world needs. We then make it possible for others to *choose us*.

When we stand up, we stand out. Think of it as sending up a smoke signal, planting a flag, or lighting a beacon. Yes, it is scary to expose ourselves by speaking out, taking our stand, or making our move. But only when we make ourselves visible do the right people for the right moment present themselves.

That's what Julie Ott learned. She and her family live in Colorado Springs and felt isolated in a town dominated by the religious right. Julie longed for a way to connect with others who shared her passion about safeguarding the environment and furthering women's rights. But with two young sons, she had scarce time for meetings. Then it dawned on Julie that she could gather allies while meeting her children's needs. She sent out a call to other mothers in the Pikes Peak Justice and Peace Commission to form a playgroup. Today it's a playgroup-cum-citizens-in-action club with ten moms and about

fifteen kids. They gather every week for several hours; the kids play, and the moms talk and scheme, read and discuss books and trade information about local political candidates.

"Several of us collaborated on a letter to the editor about the Iraq war, and it was published," Julie says. "We have real power. After all, when we write to elected officials, they don't realize that we all know each other! We live all over town, so our letters can make quite an impression." For Julie, the next step is face-to-face meetings with officials. "This group would come in handy for that.

"At Christmastime, we shared ideas for how to cut down the commercialism," Julie adds.

One mom admits that "it's been hard for me to make changes. So it felt great to hear other moms talk about how they were changing gift-giving traditions in their families."

In a downtown park in Colorado Springs on a sunny May afternoon, as I stood with Julie during the Mother's Day/Mother Earth Day celebration she'd helped to spark, I could feel her quiet satisfaction at what her "simple" act is producing. One playgroup mother told Julie that for her, it was just seeing the organic and whole foods others packed in their playgroup lunches that was the eye-opener.

GROWING A TRIBE

The sun was setting as I walked down the tree-lined Jamaica Plain streets on my way to the first members' potluck for curious minds, the network I'd been helping to create to explore and support people's unique creativity.

When I got to her home, curious minds co-founder Emily and I talked about our excitement as we waited for the first arrivals. We had no idea how many people would come, but we had decided it wouldn't really matter; we would still engage in a lively conversation over a delicious meal.

We waited. And waited. Eventually, one person showed up (and he was a friend!). That night we had an intimate three-person dinner, and Emily and I had a dose of reality, but it was not our first.

A few weeks earlier, we'd held a "Curious About Jazz" event at the Cambridge Public Library. In a private room with the capacity for at least a hundred, Emily and I waited with our presenter for an audience. That night the two of us had a very personal lecture on Miles Davis and

Wynton Marsalis, with the music echoing in the almost empty room.

We started doubting what we were doing. We believed we needed others to live creative lives, but no one seemed to want to join us. Forget about a tribe, I would have been happy with a wayward hunting party! And of course we felt fear.

But we didn't give up, though it was tempting. We started adjusting our expectations and playing with the particulars. We started having potlucks closer to where people lived, and we held them the same time every month. We rotated among different people's houses and asked people to invite their friends. We started asking ourselves what events we ourselves would want to attend. We focused on our dreams, not on what hadn't worked, and people started coming.

Now, in a break from putting the final touches on this book, I dashed out to help plan our second annual Curiosity Fair—bringing together people to informally share their stories, their passions, and their questions. It is four weeks away, and a number of details are still hanging.

Last year Emily and I took a moment before

the fair started to notice the difference: We weren't waiting for someone (anyone!) to arrive; the room was buzzing hours before the event even started, with over thirty volunteers helping us set up. By the end of the day, more than one hundred people had walked through the big doors of the YWCA to talk about their jobs, hobbies, and interests. By then Emily and I knew that by pushing through our fear, we'd built something real.

—JEFF

We are social creatures, profoundly shaped by and dependent on one another. At the same time, we are unique, each bringing distinct gifts that we often discover only in our separateness. Can we have both deep needs met—our need for inclusion *and* our need to be uniquely who we are?

Yes, but from our experience, not without risk.

When I first heard Diane Wilson speak, she was standing in front of a twenty-five-hundred-person crowd in the packed Marin convention center, an hour's drive north of San Francisco. She told of her life as a shrimper and environmentalist. To hear her bellowing voice—carrying a light Texas drawl that reminded me of my youth—

and see her vivaciousness springing from the stage, I found it hard to imagine that Diane had ever felt intimidated or shy, or doubted her strength. But Diane had come a long way to speak to us on that crisp October day.

Diane, fifty-two, was born and raised on the Gulf Coast of Texas. For four generations, her family has fished the waters off San Antonio Bay. In 1989 new environmental disclosures revealed that her county was ranked worst in the U.S. for its toxic waste. "And we're a small county," she explained, "only four towns." Seadrift has long been home to plants of some of the country's biggest chemical companies, including Formosa Plastics, DuPont, Alcoa Aluminum, and Union Carbide (now owned by Dow Chemical). Diane thought their fumes and effluent, dumped directly into the water, might have something to do with the dwindling fish populations, and she suspected they even could have caused her own son's autism.

"I was blown away, though, because I didn't see any community outrage," she said by phone from her home. "So I asked for a meeting at city hall. I reserved a room and organized it myself. When the notice went out, the mayor, county commissioners, and community leaders urged me to cancel it and let things cool down.

"I was always told to be a good girl. 'Don't say anything to upset people,' they told me."

That meeting was the beginning. She pitted herself against the region's most powerful officials and corporations. Twice her shrimp boat was sabotaged. In both instances, the bilge pump was disconnected, and bolts were loosened to create a serious leak around the propeller shaft.

"The scariest moment of my life, in 1993, was the first time they tried to get me. I was on the water, and a storm came up that made me pay attention to how low the boat was getting. Otherwise, when you're dragging your net, you might not notice. The boat could have gotten to a critical point without my knowing. That's why the water pump comes on automatically—unless it's disconnected, of course. Many a shrimper has drowned that way. I got below and saw the pump had been disconnected and worked to get the pump going. Water was spilling over the stern right above me. (And I know this sounds crazy, but I can't swim, so this was really frightening.) Any second the boat could have gone up on its stern and disappeared into that dark storm, and I knew it. But I got the pump working and the leak fixed in time and didn't go under. I would have been trapped below deck if it had." The same sabotage was tried once more, but Diane caught it before she left the dock.

Once, on a hunger strike in her own yard, a helicopter hovered low. A gunman inside shot and killed her dog and took a shot at her mother-in-law. "They were trying to scare the fire out of everybody, but I was beyond being scared."

Once she led a small group of protesters to meet a visiting Chinese industrialist from one of the polluters. They were met by three hundred hired men in hard hats. Rumor was, the men were there to make trouble, and the police weren't going to interfere. Fortunately, no one was hurt.

"The deeper I got into it, the fewer friends I had. Nobody in the three-county area would support me. My family thought I was crazy. My eldest daughter said she was going to go to work for the chemical company. The county commissioners had everyone in the area signing petitions against me. My cousin, a shrimper, went on the chemical-company payroll and spoke out against me, representing other shrimpers."

Instead of pulling back, Diane grew more determined. In a Gandhian sacrifice to demonstrate how much she cared, she planned to scuttle her forty-two-foot boat over the pipe discharging some of worst pollution into the bay. Her plan was discovered, and she was threatened with charges of terrorism on the high seas. In a raging storm, her boat was impounded and towed back to the wharf.

Then, suddenly, the winds of opinion shifted.

Other shrimpers had finally had enough, too. To protest corporate pollution, they formed a boat blockade of commercial traffic in the main channel, even though doing so was a federal crime. Vietnamese fishermen, long the shrimpers' bitter rivals, joined in, and the old foes nodded to each other across the waves. Their defiance, alongside Diane's—along with an embarrassing AP story— broke the will of the corporations. And in 1997, Formosa Plastics signed a zero-discharge agreement; Alcoa Aluminum soon followed. The agreements became a national model for environmental protection.

"Before, I was the last person you'd expect to speak out on a big issue. As a kid, I'd hide under the bed when a visitor knocked on the door. I had never even dared to speak to the manager of the bank. I doubted my own intelligence.

"But I've been a fisherman all my life, working in the elements. I've been out there when there were twisters at sea. I've been on a broke-down boat in a bad sea. I got used to risk, and I'm of the belief that if something don't kill you, it makes you stronger.

"What carried me through was that I could see what I'm doing from another perspective—like a mythical story. It's a mythical struggle. I'm just high-school-educated, but I have intuitively followed an inner voice.

I think we need to see our trials as something we have to overcome for ourselves. The struggle tells you something about your inner self. It's not just about issues; it's about your entire being. If you give up, it's not so much giving up on the issue but on yourself.

"Even when I was a little girl, I felt the bay was a person; it was like my grandmother. I don't think there's a woman alive who would give up fighting for her child, or her mother, or her grandmother—you don't give up the fight when it's for your family."

Diane got so tired at one point that she went out on the water, took too many sleeping pills, and lay down on the stern of her boat. She expected to fall into a coma-like sleep and slip into the water—home. But too many thoughts were racing in her head. "I just couldn't get to sleep. So I said the hell with it and went home and got back into the fight.

"Corporations do outrageous things, and we can see them do it—see them kill something we hold dear, inch by inch, and we sit there frozen because we're taught to sit there being well behaved.

"Why did those companies finally agree to stop polluting? They did it because I was so outrageous for so long that they could not predict or control me. They want to control every situation, and if you want to win, you have to threaten that control. I was obsessive—

three hunger strikes, and I tried to sink my shrimp boat on top of their discharge pipe. I was a threat to the predictability of their business."

The fishing industry that has supported Diane's family for so long is dying out. Mercury and other pollutants in the bay have taken their toll. (Worldwide, the picture is similar: Industrial-scale fishing has cut the population of large ocean fish by 90 percent in the last half century.[49]) But you can still find Diane out there on her little skiff. "The biggest Black Drum I caught, over limit, was a hundred pounds. I kissed it on the nose and sang it a song, 'The Yellow Rose of Texas,' and I let it go."

Was it worth it? we asked Diane.

"It was worth it. I felt stupid for a while—that's what stops many people, of course. But after you allow yourself to look stupid three or four times, you get over it.

"Sure, I've changed. My life has changed. I once told my husband, 'You know what? I like myself.' He looked at me and said that he didn't recognize me anymore and didn't much like me. I lost him and my boat and all, but I've gained so much more than I've lost because I found myself."

The path to our real home—where we are finally known and loved for the person we truly are—sometimes runs right through hell. (Remember what Winston Churchill once said about that: "If you're going through hell, keep going!") In our real home, we can count our troubles as blessings for having brought us to our new circle.

True, our strength and our challenge as human beings is that our need for connection is so intense we often go along with things that violate our own common sense, as many in Diane's town did for a long, long time. This is understandable in part when we remember that humans evolved in cultures where being cast out could literally bring death. But today in our wired (and wireless) world, we can reconstitute our tribe (we just learned there's even www.tribe.com!). We can be truer to ourselves, consciously choosing those who see us for who we are and encourage us to live our life fully.

Once the AP story about the boat blockade hit, Diane's life changed. A new community of people began to find her, people equally passionate about justice and the environment. When I saw her speak that day in October, it was at the annual gathering called Bioneers, a growing national network of ecological pioneers. She ended her speech with an adaptation of a George Bernard Shaw quote: "Look where reason has got us. A reasonable woman adapts to the world, an unreasonable woman makes the world adapt to her. What this world needs is more unreasonable women!" I jumped to my feet to join the thunderous applause.

Of that moment Diane said: "You would not believe the number of women who have told me that when my speech ended, they rushed outside with their cell phones to call friends back home, saying, 'I don't care what we start, but let's start something!'" Out of that moment sprang a network calling itself "Unreasonable Women."

Little did I know that three years later, Diane would inspire me to help create a support circle of seven women in Boston, calling ourselves Unreasonable Women.

"So many people have lost faith in themselves," Diane said. "I offer a chance to believe again. But I am a poor woman, no education, nobody in particular. If I can do it, anybody can. People see that. We're all taught to be too well behaved. Thoreau said on his deathbed: 'The only thing I regret was that I was too well behaved.'"

Countless ripples have come out of Diane's call, including the birth of her own tribe. Recently, she pledged a thirty-day hunger strike to protest Dow Chemical's refusal to accept responsibility for a 1984 chemical disaster in Bhopal, India, caused by a company they now own, Union Carbide. In the past, Diane's hunger strikes were lonely affairs. This time Unreasonable Women friends and coconspirators from around the country flocked to her side. They took turns joining her in her flatbed truck under the hot Texas sun, greeting Dow workers as they entered the plant.

Diane's story reminds us that we are all free to create our own tribes, and that we have almost unlimited opportunities to do so—with potentially good friends, old and new, popping out of what we mistook to be the thin air of a frightening void. We can also feel compassion for ourselves, knowing that our bodies—including our fear responses—are still influenced mightily by prehistoric wiring. Even if our biological systems have not yet received the news that things have changed, with compassion we can take the risks we must in order to create *new* responses, gradually cluing our bodies in to the new day that's dawning.

OLD THOUGHT	NEW THOUGHT
If I'm really myself, I'll be excluded. If I break connection, I'll be alone forever.	To find genuine connection, we must risk disconnection. The new light we shine draws others toward us, and we become conscious choosers.

Women in the Rain

On Multiplying Courage

frankie Thirty years ago, Women Strike for Peace helped achieve a remarkable victory: an end to the above-ground nuclear testing that rained radioactive fallout worldwide, even showing up at dangerous levels in mothers' milk. Journalist Rebecca Solnit recalls hearing a middle-aged member of the group talking about feeling utterly "foolish and futile" as she stood in the rain one morning, sign in hand, protesting at the Kennedy White House.[50]

Futile? Many years later, she would hear Dr. Benjamin Spock—then one of the country's highest-profile opponents of nuclear testing—say that the turning-to-action point for him was seeing a small group of women standing in the rain, protesting at the White House. According to Solnit, Spock concluded: "If they were so passionately committed, he should give the issue more consideration himself."

"It's always too early to calculate effect," Solnit warned us, yet that's exactly what we grasp for: We want to know we're making a difference. We fear our own insignificance. Looking back, I know that was the fear that pushed me out of grad school to seek my path. Yet too frequently, this kind of fear isn't motivating; it's debilitating. How often do we hear friends and acquaintances lament their drop-in-the-bucket status, their feeling of powerlessness.

The consequences of such internal messages are momentous. But we don't realize just how momentous until we think of what's possible when people believe the opposite. Call up in your mind one of those dramatic scenes we've all heard about, when someone marshals the strength of Hercules to lift a three-thousand-pound car off a trapped child, or when someone rushes without a moment's hesitation into a burning building to save a stranger. Where do they find the strength and courage?

In part, these qualities appear because at such moments, people know their actions matter—*really* matter. Imagine if you and I could see that our actions can matter that much; if we were to carry within us the understanding that our small planet, down to our own community, *is* that burning building. And like the people in these life-and-death encounters, we know it's up to us and no one else to save the day. Raw energy could burst forth to carry us through our fear.

I recall my first inkling of this energy shift. I was thirty-one years old, flying back from Rome, where I'd attended the first United Nations conference to end hunger. I'd gone mainly to learn. But to my astonishment, the "expert" corporate and government heads were trapped in the myths that I'd discovered were actually blinding us to the solutions at hand. I still recall the flight home, reclining in my airplane seat, thinking, Oh my God, this means it is up to me. If not me, who?

This didn't feel like an ego-centered thought, but more like an awakening to an essential truth. The depth, pervasiveness, and complexity of today's problems mean that answers can't come from the top down; they have to come from the bottom up, from "regular" people acting on common sense and assuming responsibility. Suddenly, my energy surged; I knew exactly what I had to do when I got home. In record time, I rewrote my first book, *Diet for a Small Planet,* making its message even clearer and ultimately reaching millions of readers.

The opposite, an energy sink, is what happens when a tiny dribble into a lousy bucket is all we imagine ourselves to be. In order to stop disempowering ourselves, it might help to dissect the thoughts wrapped up inside the deadly drop-in-the-bucket refrain. One is the notion that we are oddballs if we care about others and the larger world; that we are misfits because we want more from our lives than survival and material ease.

This idea is deflating, because if we really believe we're so unusual, how can we imagine a significantly better world emerging? Impossible! There are too few of us to bring it into being.

We can let go of this thought trap pretty easily once we acknowledge the obvious: that if human beings didn't have the twin needs for connection with one another and effectiveness in the outer world, we wouldn't have made it this far. (Admittedly, at six billion plus, we've yet to achieve the biomass of ants, but it's nonetheless a remarkable evolutionary triumph.[51]) We're hardwired, as the opening chapter notes, to enjoy cooperating with one another. In fact, we're hardwired to care, as are our nearest relatives in the animal kingdom.

In one experiment, researchers noted that rhesus monkeys "abstained from pulling a chain that would deliver food to them if pulling the chain also caused another monkey to receive an electric shock. Some monkeys would not eat for hours, or even days."[52] Yes, of course, rhesus monkeys and human beings can be made to override our consideration for others. At least with humans, it happens all the time. But that fact in no way denies our innate caring; it only tells us that mighty forces are at work, pressuring us to do the opposite—to pull that chain.

A survey of more than three thousand Americans found—as many of us have discovered on our own— what researchers call a "helper's high." Ninety-five percent of volunteers reported that after helping others, they feel better physically and emotionally. They reported heightened energy and feelings of greater serenity.[53]

That anyone would be surprised by these findings is what should give us pause, alerting us to the power of ubiquitous false messages about who we are. Related is the widespread assumption that in disasters, human beings are bound to panic, thinking only of saving our own necks. We'd trample our own grandmas if we had to! "Dead wrong," researcher Lee Clark has said. Five decades of studying scores of disasters, such as floods, earthquakes, and tornadoes, show that "people rarely lose control."[54] Since the media focuses on the exceptions, we come to believe they are the rule. In catastrophes, as we saw on September 11, individuals "are more likely to engage in altruistic behaviors than egoistic behaviors and to do so with proximate strangers as well as with their own companions," said sociologist Clark McPhail, who has studied this question for years.[55]

Since caring about something beyond ourselves is natural, it follows that the real oddballs are those who aren't in touch with such feelings. How much more empowering is that thought! It follows, then, that witnessing another's pain but *not* acting—as we do, for example, in walking with eyes diverted past a destitute hungry person—violates not just some abstract, unheeded "you should," but something much deeper inside us.

Since we evolved in close-knit tribes, utterly dependent on one another, it makes perfect sense that values fostering the group's welfare became part of what we call human nature. But with the so-called culture wars at home, and the tumult over an apparent chasm between the Islamic worldview and the West's, any notion of common values seems easily tossed out as a pipe dream. If there are no common values, where's the basis for common problem solving?

Rushmore Kidder, founder of the Institute for Global Ethics in Maine, begs to differ. His *Shared Values for a Troubled World* reviewed his conversations with diverse people from widely differing world cultures and identified many underlying values they all share. Among them are truthfulness, fairness, responsibility, and respect for life.[56] Adam Smith himself, supposedly the godfather of dog-eat-dog (aka valueless) economics, believed that all humanity shares a number of deeply rooted moral sentiments. He singled out justice, noting a "remarkable distinction" between it and other "social virtues." Other virtues are somewhat optional, but "we feel ourselves to be in a peculiar manner tied, bound, and obliged to the observation of justice."[57]

Here, too, with our sharp sense of fairness, we're not alone in the animal world. In a recent experiment, capuchin monkeys flatly refused rewards when they saw other monkeys favored with tastier ones. (The scientists, I was amused to note, seemed reluctant to use positive language, calling the behavior "inequity aversion."[58]) Even vampire bats and ravens detect overeaters among those gathering the food, and punish the cheaters.[59]

Perhaps we humans, and other animals, too, feel so deeply about justice or fairness because we evolved knowing that infractions against it weaken community on which our lives depend. As Smith noted, it is injustice that "will utterly destroy" society.

———

But the drop-in-the-bucket mind-set, leading so many to despair of ever making real change in the world, is even more debilitating than we might think. We may *say* we feel like a drop in the bucket, but egad, we feel more like drops in the Sahara, evaporating even before hitting the sand. We feel this way, totally insignificant, because we can't see the bucket.

To flip our fear of insignificance into surging power, we must be able to perceive that bucket: the wider pattern of positive change that our efforts help bring to life. The fact is, buckets fill up pretty fast, as anyone knows who's ever had a leaky roof on a rainy night.

Intriguingly, the last few decades have seen revolutions in our perceptions of reality that make this trick much more possible. Many born since the 1960s, for example, may not realize that the very word "ecology" is brand-new to popular language. What is ecology, anyway? It's the science of relationships—of the intricate webs linking all of life—that is gradually infusing our consciousness. Advances not just in natural history but in math, computers, and physics allow us to see interconnections we could not see before.

In his book *Linked*, Albert-László Barabási, a physics professor at Notre Dame, wrote: "We have come to see that we live in a small world, where everything is linked to everything else."[60] If we let this simple fact sink in, we realize how much power we have. Networks are key to understanding the world, Barabási added. "Small changes . . . affecting only a few of the nodes or links can open up hidden doors, allowing new possibilities to emerge."[61] We despair over our individual powerlessness only if we remain trapped in our own skins and blind to the intricate networks sewing us all together. In networks, every one of us is a "node" whose actions can ripple through all the links.

Not only are we all woven in multiple networks, but Barabási showed that the clichéd "six degrees of separation" is much more significant than the occasional aha on finding that the person next to you on the plane went to grade school with your ex-boyfriend. There is a shockingly short pathway among us all. Even on the Internet, with its billion nodes, any document, Barabási recounted, is only nineteen clicks from any other.[62]

Once seeing the world as a closely woven net, not a bunch of discrete boxes, our perception of our own actions in the world shifts. The old notion, for example, that positive outcomes result from citizens and do-good groups tackling issues can seem overwhelming. There are just too many, and more seem to crop up every day. The problem is that we imagine an issue as something we can separate out, with a beginning and ending: issues like child care, water pollution, gay rights, money's influence in politics, and so on. But actually, there are no issues, distinct and finite. There are only entry points into the network of life. If we think of our actions as entry points, each affecting a node in the pattern, then we see we are in fact shifting the whole pattern when we act with clear intention. The ripples through the network are potentially infinite. What a sense of power!

THE RIPPLES OF OUR COURAGE

Tonight I called my mother. I wanted to talk about how my coming out five years ago had affected her life. At first she didn't want to talk because she'd miss Richard Chamberlain on *Larry King Live,* talking about coming out as a gay man. "I love it when people come out about who they are," she said.

Soon after I came out, my mother wanted to learn what it meant to be the mother of a gay child, so she started going to meetings of the local PFLAG (Parents, Families and Friends of Lesbians and Gays).

"At the time I got your letter, I felt sad, hurt,

and angry, but I couldn't share the loss with others. We had lost the son we thought we had, and now we had to find our true son. Through PFLAG, I found a safe space to share these feelings and thoughts. I found I wasn't alone. It wasn't long before I was asked to join the New Hampshire PFLAG board, where I found so many wonderful people who share a common concern for the GLBT community."

Now she is co–vice president of the state board of PFLAG.

"When I speak to groups, especially students, I tell them that what I say may not apply to their lives today, but someday they may have a friend, relative, child, or grandchild who will need their support and love because they are gay, lesbian, bisexual, transgendered, or questioning."

Last year she flew, for only the second time in her life, to the national PFLAG conference in Ohio, and she's already planning a trip to next year's conference in Utah. Recently, she marched with other New Hampshire parents in the Boston Pride Parade, wearing a button: "I love my gay son, two straight daughters, and three grandchildren."

"I love marching in the parade. I don't feel like I am necessarily representing you, but rather, it is like I am someone else's mom that day. I'm there for the kids who come out whose parents reject them. It is so freeing to see people being true to themselves. We are always well received. So many people come up to us and thank us for marching. They say they wished their parents were as accepting."

During the 1960s, my mom had longed to take part in the civil rights movement in the South, to help register voters during Freedom Summer. But her parents refused to let her go; they were too frightened for her safety.

She hardly could have guessed that forty years later, having a gay son would allow her to become a campaigner for civil rights. Rather than working in the South for the rights of African-Americans, she speaks in rural New Hampshire towns about gays' and lesbians' need to enjoy equal rights.

"This spring Judy Shepard, mother of Matthew Shepard [murdered in 1998 for being gay], came to our town," she said, "to speak about how we all need to be out and talk about these issues. We can't be afraid to talk about these things, because when we talk, we make it easier for others. She is an inspiration to any parent."

Finding my voice, it turned out, allowed my mother to find hers. Now she is more up on gay politics than I am. Saying good night, I can't help but notice the difference between this call and the fateful one I made five years ago. So much has changed. —JEFF

When I set out to dig up the roots of hunger, my search led me to the economic givens creating deprivation alongside surplus: I saw more and more grain going to livestock (now over 40 percent worldwide) to produce meat for the planet's better off, because so many people are too poor to buy the grain for their own consumption. I began to see that what I put in my mouth is not a separate health issue; it directly affects everything from hunger to the long-term viability of our soil to global warming, since fossil-fuel-consuming agriculture is a top contributor of greenhouse gases. Our everyday food choices have endless ripples.

But the ripple metaphor takes us only partway. Our ripples don't dwindle as they expand toward the shore.

They converge, creating waves, sometimes crashing through dikes of resistance. As Malcolm Gladwell wrote in his popular *The Tipping Point,* change can build slowly until suddenly there's a breakthrough moment when something takes off—the "tipping point." It's the positive version of the straw breaking the camel's back; we just lack an aphorism to make clear that this phenomenon can work for positive change as well.

Since no one can predict a tipping point, we'll never know whether our action might be the straw. I think, for instance, of when my daughter and I were in Brazil with leaders of a successful movement of over two million poor, landless people. The last thing we expected was to hear that Cesar Chavez's farmworkers' movement, six thousand miles away in California, had helped inspire the birth of their movement—one that has drastically reduced infant deaths and created thousands of schools and tens of thousands of jobs in new communities throughout almost every state in Brazil.

None of us ever knows who's watching.

Earlier we said that being able to perceive the bucket is key to seeing our power. To know that our drops don't just evaporate in the desert is to gain hope, transmuting fear to positive energy.

What is that bucket we're filling? The vessel that holds our conscious choices and allows them to collect is not, we're convinced, a particular issue, such as a campaign to save the environment; nor is it a new political "ism" defining a better society. The bucket is an awakening, a set of new, complementary perceptions of reality that themselves make movement toward a more life-serving planet conceivable. One we just mentioned is the perception at life as a network instead of as a set of isolated issues.

Another is a new understanding of power: what it is and who has it. We've lived for so long under the spell of hierarchy—from god-kings to feudal lords to party bosses—that only in the last few hundred years has the mist begun to clear. In this country, it's because certain among us have been willing to walk with fear to dump tea into a harbor, to stand up against slavery, to march down the street claiming that even females could be trusted with the vote, and to sit in at lunch counters in Mississippi.

We're coming to see that one Sally Riggs, trained and backed by skilled allies, is more powerful than a hundred mortgage executives. One Diane Wilson, once her courage moved her fellow shrimpers and fishermen, is more powerful than an industrial empire. A few women in the rain are more powerful than government leaders. With "regular people" like Sally Riggs or Jack Shipley, Julie Ott or Willie Manteris stepping out in their communities—becoming knowledgeable in arcane matters of finance and forest fires and foreign policy— our expectations change about the legitimate role of citizens, those without official authority.

This radical shift in perception is so pervasive, happening on so many levels, that it's hard to identify it for the revolution it is. Some measure it in the explosive growth of citizen organizations, now totaling two million in the U.S. alone and growing worldwide, too.[63] In just one decade, the '90s, they jumped 60 percent![64] And they're being noticed: More national governments, as well as the UN, are inviting citizen representatives to the table. This growing appreciation of the power of regular people also means some students gaining a role in school governance. Work teams spreading in factories. Citizen assemblies in major municipalities now making significant budget choices. And patients increasingly enlisted in their own healing practice. Everywhere, people are coming to understand that the more participants get involved in decisions affecting their futures, the better the outcomes are for all.[65]

Here again, we humans are more like our animal friends than we might have guessed. Animal-behavior experts long assumed that, say, the head-honcho buffalo decides when the herd moves, but now they're discovering it doesn't work that way. Such actions reflect the preference of the majority. For instance, red deer, native to Britain, move only when 60 percent of the adults stand up. Whooper swans of northern Europe "vote" by moving their heads; African buffalo, by the direction of the females' gaze. Scientists also conclude that this sort of animal democracy carries a tangible survival edge over top-down direction.[66]

Putting this all together, we see that rather than inhabiting a top-down, command-and-control world, where those at the bottom have virtually no power, we are living in a highly interconnected world with changes rippling up and through billions of "nodes"—that's us and our communities.

If this is true, how do we come to feel it in our bones? If mirror neurons exist, as the previous chapter celebrated, then we can become aware from moment to moment that our daily actions help to create what goes on around us. Mirror neurons mean that we influence one another in ways mysterious and invisible: When I'm watching your actions, my brain fires as if I'm taking those actions myself. We are forever sending signals. In *The Sense of Being Stared At,* Cambridge University biologist Rupert

Sheldrake offered intriguing evidence that such an exchange goes on beneath conscious awareness.[67]

We must not forget that our actions send signals to ourselves, too. To transform our fear of insignificance, we must ride herd on those messages. While we may *want* to believe the world can change, how can we possibly believe that others more oppressed—some pushed to the very edge of survival—can find their voices if we don't experience ourselves changing? Or, to state it positively: We can believe the world can change only as we experience *ourselves* changing. Ultimately, our own direct experience is the most convincing.

At the end of our lives, few of us want to meet an unchanged self. Don't we hope to discover that who we are has changed many times throughout our lives, as we learned to listen and to respond in new ways to the unknown?

There may be just one sure way to realize that hope. It is, as we've noted, being willing to risk. Risk is anything that brings up fear. What feels like a risk to one of us may feel like a breeze to you. Yet as we see ourselves doing what we thought we could not do, we become what we all secretly want to be: heroes to ourselves. We feel more powerful. And we are.

Recalling the terror that I felt three years ago in relocating to a new city and taking on a five-continent journey to write *Hope's Edge,* I recognize that having simply put myself in that uncomfortable-for-me circumstance generated interior changes. I am not exactly the same person I was then. As I absorb the shock of breast cancer and treatment while pressing another book deadline, it all seems imminently doable—or at least it does at this moment!

More dramatically, compare the timid and frightened Sally Riggs to the Sally who addressed a conference of two thousand people; compare the young Diane Wilson who hid under the bed when guests arrived to the Diane standing up to corporate giants. As they did what they once believed impossible, they experienced themselves as different, more powerful people.

There were times in Guatemala, George Leger told us, when "I felt like I was drowning. I remember one particular night when I felt I could no longer face the suffering. It all seemed just too hopeless. But I soon realized that if I hung in there, I would in time be able to better handle so harsh a reality. If just one person tries to respond to a heartbreaking situation, that itself is reason to hope. If I turned my back on the situation, that, at least for me, would make it seem hopeless."

George's resolve gave him hope; in a sense, his connection with other people's suffering served his own happiness. That's just how human beings are wired.

———

As we proceed on our walk with fear, we become more convincing to ourselves, and we can look out to the rest of the world, able to see possibilities once hidden from view. Others also see our courage growing, and we can never guess the impact. So as you begin to embrace new, liberating thoughts about fear, one thing is certain: Your change does not stop with you.

OLD THOUGHT	NEW THOUGHT
I'm just a drop in the bucket. My effort might make me feel better, but it can't do much.	Every time we act, even with our fear, we make room for others to do the same. Courage is contagious.

Fear, Courage, and Hope

W e're finishing our book on Labor Day weekend—how appropriate. Our book is all about labor, about our inner and outer work. It is about the work of looking at our own lives, our most daily decisions. Only here can we find the answer to the biggest question of this historic moment, when fear and hope seem to wrestle inside us: To which will we listen?

This choice fills our book.

On the one hand, we can see our fears as our own private trials and tell ourselves that we are just not risk takers; other people are. We can leave the future to them and tell ourselves that we're just here to get by, to make it through. We can wait for someone else to speak, for someone else to create.

Or we can open ourselves to discover something new about who we are and why we're here. We can feel fear not as a sign of danger but as a signal that we're on the edge of something beautiful whose shape is still unformed.

Certainly, staying trapped in the false messages of the dominant tribe doesn't mean our lives are easy. Hardly. We look around and see millions of Americans strangled by debt, as Sally Riggs found herself, or working longer and longer hours at work that leaves one "totally spent each day," as Willie Manteris felt, "barely able to make it into the house."

When we choose to be true to ourselves, something new emerges, not only transforming our own lives but touching untold numbers of others. The meaning of fear changes as well.

"There is a certain threshold that you cross," Willie says, referring to his own journey to do what he believed was important. "Once you do that, you see a different world. I'm not afraid of the old fears anymore. I'm in a different world.

"Everyone asked about my trips to Central America: 'Was it dangerous, were you afraid?' The fact is, there are dangers, but they have a different meaning. You see the conditions of the people. You see the absolute heroism of the workers helping; you see possibility. So if some kind of harm comes to you, it's not as important."

One might think that the choices of the people in our book bring heaviness into their lives—isn't suffering inevitable in working against high odds? That's not what we've found in our lives or in the lives of others. As we learn to walk with fear, we become filled with hope, not wishful thinking but honest hope. We learn that it's impossible to *find* hope; we can only *become* it. That's what the people in this book are saying to us all. We become hope, with all its wonderment and surprise, as we act, as we walk with fear, fear of being out of step, looking foolish, being rejected or even killed.

We despair over the world and our individual powerlessness only if we stay trapped inside our own skins, unable to see the intricate networks weaving us together. But as the lives of the people in this book show so clearly—from Valarie and Diane to Arn and Julie—a worldwide quickening is under way of bottom-up, life-enhancing change in which we each can find ourselves, and in which we can each find joy.

We like to call it living democracy because it feels alive—an ongoing creation, not an end point. Once appreciating our connections, we know we have the power. We can celebrate the new life emerging, as even across continents, more and more people are motivating one another to walk with fear, transforming its energy to create the world we want.

I would like to beg you, dear Sir, as well as I can, to have patience with everything unresolved in your heart and try to love *the questions themselves* as if they were locked rooms or books written in a very foreign language. Don't search for answers, which could not be given to you now, because you would not be able to live them. And the point is, to live everything. *Live* the questions now. Perhaps then, someday far in the future, you will gradually, without even noticing it, live your way into the answer.

—FROM *Letters to a Young Poet,*
RAINER MARIA RILKE[68]

Choosing Courage

Ideas for Discussion and Action

*W*e've found that facing our fear is a lot easier if we have companions on the journey. Community itself is a powerful tool in transforming fear. For Frankie, the Kay-yakers offered a cove of nurturance, giving her the opportunity to explore the ideas in this book. For Jeff, the curious minds network continues to push him to shed the seven old thoughts in favor of the seven liberating ones.

We've raised some of the biggest questions of our lives: What do we fear? What do we dream? Where do we find meaning? Sometimes the best way to grapple with these questions is to discuss them with others. In the next few pages, you'll find questions for reading groups, as well as ideas for starting Courage Circles of your own, and more personal questions to explore with a group or on your own. Consider these a jumping-off point.

You can find more resources and communicate with us through our website: www.uhavethepower.org. We'd love to hear from you. Please tell us how you're using *You Have the Power,* the questions you're asking, and the discoveries you're making.

Thank you for reading our book, and thank you for tackling what may be life's toughest challenge. Thank you for multiplying courage.   —FRANKIE AND JEFF

Reading Group Discussion Questions

1. In "Dark Matter," Frankie mentions the mythological and religious traditions of "facing the void"—the voyage through the desert, the retreat to the cave. What learning have you experienced in being alone? What new ideas do you have about silence?

2. Frankie talks about walking into thin air in "The Kayakers' Cove." What does this expression mean to you? Have you had experiences that felt like you were walking into thin air? When? What did they feel like?

3. Woody Allen says, "Ninety percent of life is showing up" (or at least something like that!). The authors explore the idea that we don't need to conquer our fears in order to take on new challenges: "We don't have to believe we can do it to do it," they write. "The

very act of showing up, even with our fear, has power." What do they mean by "showing up"? Have you found this concept to be true in your own life? If so, in what ways?

4. How do you define conflict? What new lessons about conflict did you discover in "The Fires of Creation"? What do you think about viewing creative conflict as an art?

5. In "The Fires of Creation," Herb Walters says that "listening is a bridge across . . . fears." Can you think of a time when active listening had such an effect for you? Or when it could have had such an effect?

6. In "The Dragon's Mouth," Jeff describes a nightmare in which a monster chases him and he wakes up in a cold sweat. Do you have a recurring dream about fear? How might you "fly into the monster's mouth," as Jeff described doing?

7. In "The Kayakers' Cove," what does the cove represent for Frankie? Do you have such a place or community in your life?

8. In "Women in the Rain," the authors suggest that it's never possible to predict the impact of our actions. How can we know when we ourselves might

be the tipping point? The authors describe the rainy-day Women Strike for Peace protest on the steps of the Kennedy White House. Only years later did one of the participants learn that her action was influential in Dr. Benjamin Spock's ardent opposition to above-ground nuclear testing. Discuss the idea of the ripple effect and the tipping point. Can you think of positive versions of the straw that broke the camel's back?

9. Flutist and survivor of Cambodian genocide Arn Chorn-Pond says, "Before, I was forced to live in fear; now I choose." What can Arn's story teach us about the choice to live in fear or not?

10. Consider the story of Diane Wilson. What do you think gave her the courage to take on some of the world's largest chemical corporations?

11. The authors argue that most of us—not just an idealistic few—want to experience lives of meaning, to feel our existence matters. Do you agree?

12. Rainer Maria Rilke says in the book's opening quote: "Perhaps everything that frightens us is, in its deepest essence, something helpless that wants our love." What does this mean to you? What might this mean in your life?

13. The importance of tribe runs throughout the book. In the opening chapter, the authors talk about the "hyper-tribe" as a globe-spanning "corporate-controlled culture" on a "competitive treadmill." What does this mean to you? What evidence of this have you seen in your own life? What is your tribe? What values would you like your tribe to foster, and what qualities would you like your tribe to support in you?

14. Tribes can be either limiting or freeing. How can we be sure our chosen tribes don't cut us off from those outside but rather support us in connecting with those unlike ourselves?

15. The authors write: "Imprintability itself is a source of hope; we 'become' each other in some mysterious way, and it happens without our even knowing." How have you been "imprinted" by others, positively or negatively? Have your ideas of hope changed in reading this book?

16. The book ends by arguing that only by walking with our fears can we create a true, living democracy. Do you agree? In what ways do talking about fear and learning to face our fears bring us closer to a living democracy?

17. Think about the role of the media in creating fear. Discuss specific examples of fear-provoking media that you've seen recently. What would a "hope news" media diet mean in your life?

18. Refer to the chart "Seven Old Thoughts and Seven New Thoughts About Fear" (see page 189). Read each aloud and discuss your reactions.

Creating Your Own Courage Circles

For those who would like to engage in an ongoing conversation about an evolving relationship with fear, we offer these suggestions and questions for reflection.

Ideas for Courage Circles

- Reflect on how you may want to begin your group sessions: maybe in silence. Maybe with a writing exercise. Maybe with a fear check-in, describing what is causing anxiety or fear at that moment.

- Consider supporting one another in journal keeping, regularly answering some of the questions on the next few pages in your journal and reflecting back with the group on changes and learning.

- Beyond discussing these questions and recording your reflections in a journal, you may want to invite one another to help ignite the fires of creation through role-playing and active listening around particularly challenging conflicts.

- Exchange recommendations of other ideas, books, resources, films, and songs that expand your ideas of the possible.

- Think about ending each gathering by recounting an act of courage one of you has witnessed, expanding everyone's sense of the possible.

We offer the following questions as touchstones on your journey. You'll have your own. As you proceed, you may feel astonished that what once seemed daunting has lost its sting.

Reflection Questions

These questions are meant to be used however they best serve you, either answering them on your own, in a journal, or in a Courage Circle.

1. What happened today or in the last week that brought up fear? Could I see this fear as a signal that I am on new ground?

2. What were my physical sensations, and where were they? What was my response to these feelings? What is one thing I could do differently in the future?

3. What did I do today or this week that took courage—maybe not for anyone else, but for me? Was it expressing a criticism? Asking for something I needed? Acknowledging to someone a feeling that before I might have tried to hide? Walking into an unknown situation?

4. What did I do today or this week to bring images of possibility into my life? Read an article or a book? Meet a person? Hear or see a radio report, film, website?

5. How much time did I spend by myself this week? What kind of chatter went on in my head during that time? Did it feel uncomfortable to be alone? What did I do with that discomfort? When I was by myself, what were my sources of pleasure?

6. How do I deal with conflict in my life? What is my first response? Have I ever experienced conflict as constructive?

7. What has been one of my most difficult life

experiences? Was this something I feared? In what ways was it my teacher?

8. What was my childhood experience with fear? What was I afraid of? How have the things I fear changed?

9. If I were to "come out" as myself to those around me, what might be some of the important parts of me that people don't know?

10. Who are the members of my "tribe"? Do I feel supported by those members to be real about who I am?

11. From whom do I want to learn? Who gives me courage? What can I learn from their lives?

12. Whom do I know doing something I believe in? How could I arrange my life to be around that person more often?

13. With whom do I now spend time? Are they doing what they really want to do? What are their fears? Might I help them talk about their dreams?

14. Are there people in my life holding me back, sending negative messages, telling me that change is too risky? What can I do to let go of their influence?

15. What is one thing I've never done that I've always

been curious about that I can start now? What is a first step?

16. What negative thoughts keep me from walking toward my dream? What new, empowering thoughts can I put in their place right now?

Seven Old Thoughts and Seven New Thoughts About Fear

OLD THOUGHTS	NEW THOUGHTS
Fear means I'm in danger. Something's wrong. I must escape and seek safety.	Fear is pure energy. It's a signal. It might not mean stop, it could mean go!
If I stop what I'm doing, I'll be lost, I'll never start again.	Sometimes we have to stop in order to find our path.
I have to figure it all out before I can do anything.	We don't have to believe we can do it to do it; the very act of showing up, even with our fear, has power.

OLD THOUGHTS	NEW THOUGHTS
If I act on what I believe, I fear conflict will break out. I'll be humiliated, ineffective, and rejected.	Conflict means engagement. Something real is in motion. It's an opening, not a closing.
Our greatest fears are our worst enemies; they drag us down and hold us back.	Our worst fears can be our greatest teachers.
If I'm really myself, I'll be excluded. If I break connection, I'll be alone forever.	To find genuine connection, we must risk disconnection. The new light we shine draws others toward us, and we become conscious choosers.
I'm just a drop in the bucket. My effort might make me feel better, but it can't do much.	Every time we act, even with our fear, we make room for others to do the same. Courage is contagious.

Recommended Reading

THE ARTIST'S WAY: A SPIRITUAL PATH TO HIGHER CREATIVITY
Julia Cameron (New York: J. P. Tarcher/Putnam, 1992)

A twelve-week program to find meaning and creativity in your life. Great to use in a group.

THE ART OF POSSIBILITY: TRANSFORMING PROFESSIONAL AND PERSONAL LIFE
Benjamin and Rosamund Stone Zander (Boston: Harvard Business School Press, 2000)

Paradigm-shifting ideas and simple illustrations help you move from limits to possibilities.

FEEL THE FEAR AND DO IT ANYWAY
Susan Jeffers (New York: Fawcett Books, 1992)

Focused on fears in work and personal life, this classic offers a plan for moving forward with fear.

Freeing the Soul from Fear
Robert Sardello (New York: Riverhead, 1999)

A profound exploration of the relationship of fear and love

Hope's Edge: The Next Diet for a Small Planet
Frances Moore Lappé and Anna Lappé (New York: J. P. Tarcher/Putnam, 2002)

The Lappés explore fear and hope through stories of courageous change-makers on five continents. Includes one hundred pages of vegetarian recipes from the country's leading restaurateurs and cookbook authors.

An Intimate History of Humanity
Theodore Zeldin (New York: HarperCollins, 1994)

An internationally renowned historian looks beneath traditional concepts of history and finds a new, hopeful perspective.

Let Your Life Speak: Listening for the Voice of Vocation
Parker J. Palmer (San Francisco: Jossey-Bass, 2000)

Thoughts on what it means to listen to oneself and create space for the soul to speak its truth

Making a Living While Making a Difference
Melissa Everett (Gabriola Island, BC, Canada: New Society Press, 1999)

A practical guide on creating careers with a conscience. Includes a ten-step process for career development.

Man's Search for Meaning
Viktor Frankl (New York: Touchstone, 1984, originally published in 1946)

Pioneering work about Frankl's experiences in Nazi concentration camps and the insights he gained

Mindfulness
Ellen Langer (Cambridge, Mass.: Perseus Publishing, 1989)

Helps us understand how we get caught in mindlessness and dramatically shows the power of our thoughts.

Mourning Has Broken: Learning from the Wisdom of Adversity
Carmella B'Hahn (Bath, UK: Crucible, 2002)

Using interviews and stories as examples, offers eight keys to working with our most difficult experiences.

No Death No Fear: Comforting Wisdom for Life
Thich Nhat Hanh (New York: Riverhead, 2002)

World-renowned Vietnamese monk Thich Nhat

Hanh offers Buddhist wisdom on transforming grief and fear.

WHEN THINGS FALL APART: HEART ADVICE FOR DIFFICULT TIMES
Pema Chödrön (Boston: Shambhala, 2000)

Essays helping us see that what scares us is what provides our opportunity for awakening

THE WISDOM OF INSECURITY
Alan Watts (New York: Vintage, 1951)

A great reminder that all of life is uncertain; it challenges us to use uncertainty as a tool for deeper living.

ZEN AND THE ART OF MAKING A LIVING
Laurence G. Boldt (New York: Penguin, 1999)

Hands-on resources dedicated to helping you find meaningful work

Selected Resources for a "Hope News" Diet

News of inspiring action as well as in-depth coverage and penetrating analysis

Magazines: A Sampling

HOPE
Web: www.hopemag.com
Phone: 800-273-7447

Six times a year, *Hope* brings you a treasure trove of stories about struggle, innovation, and surprise—stories about ordinary people doing the extraordinary, tackling tough challenges in every walk of life.

RESURGENCE
Rocksea Farmhouse, St. Mabyn, Bodmin, Cornwall
PL30 3BR

Web: http:resurgence.gn.apc.org/

Published in the UK, *Resurgence,* under the leadership of visionary Satish Kumar, is a moving and beautiful mix of outstanding photography, artwork, and penetrating essays—new thinking in ecology, spirituality, and community-based economics.

UTNE

Web: www.utne.com

Phone: 800-736-UTNE

Bimonthly, *Utne* reprints the best articles from more than two thousand alternative media sources, bringing you the latest ideas and trends emerging in our culture. Also boasts active online discussion.

WORLDWATCH

Web: www.worldwatch.org

This highly readable bimonthly magazine keeps you up on global trends and breakthroughs related to water, soil, food, climate change, species extinction, and other challenges, as well as innovative solutions.

YES!

Web: www.futurenet.org

Phone: 800-937-4451

A quarterly, *Yes!* connects readers to a community of change-makers. Each issue focuses on a theme, showing the possibilities and practical steps that can lead us all to a more positive future.

Check Out These News and Opinion Websites to Take You Behind the Sound Bites:

- www.gnn.tv: The news site of Frankie's son, Anthony Lappé, and colleagues at the Guerrilla News Network. Original interviews and analysis, along with critical republished articles and active online discussion. Known for dynamic news videos and Sundance-winning short documentaries.

- www.tompaine.com: A range of progressive opinion pieces, book news, and more.

- www.commondreams.com: Breaking news and commentary from the progressive community.

- www.idealist.org: Though considered primarily a source for nonprofit jobs and volunteer opportunities, this website features articles that focus on grassroots efforts underneath the headlines.

- www.christiansciencemonitor.com: The website of *The Christian Science Monitor* provides domestic and international news that often includes stories of innovative solutions to public problems.

The Authors' Work

CURIOUS MINDS
617-864-3934
P.O. Box 382281, Cambridge, MA 02238

Jeff cofounded this community initiative, bringing together people who support one another in finding their life's work. Jeff and his colleagues hope curious minds will inspire similar local initiatives across the country. See their website, www.curiousminds.org, to find out what they've done in Boston.

SMALL PLANET INSTITUTE
617-441-6300, ext. 115
25 Mount Auburn Street, Cambridge, MA 02138
www.smallplanetinstitute.org

Frances, a small staff, and collaborators worldwide—including her children, Anthony Lappé (www.gnn.tv) and Anna Lappé (anna@smallplanetfund.org)—create books, speeches, articles, workshops, an e-mail newsletter, multimedia presentations, and a fund (www.smallplanetfund.org) supporting democratic movements in the book *Hope's Edge*. Our goal is to help people create frameworks of understanding and find personal entry points so that we can be powerful creators of the world they want.

**A Selection of Organizations Related to
the People and Themes of the Book:**

Diane Wilson's organization: CALHOUN COUNTY
RESOURCE WATCH
361-785-3907
Box 1001, Seadrift, TX 77983

Works to protect Texas bays and rivers and further a
sustainable environment, including the well-being of
the community and chemical workers and fishermen.

Arn Chorn-Pond is artistic director of CAMBODIAN
MASTER PERFORMERS PROGRAM
617-482-9485
44 Farnsworth Street, Boston, MA 02210
http://www.cambodianmasters.org

A project of the nonprofit World Education, the
program supports the revival of traditional art forms in
Cambodia as well as inspires contemporary artistic
expression.

Jeff's mother's work: PARENTS, FAMILIES AND
FRIENDS OF LESBIANS AND GAYS (PFLAG)
202-467-8180
1726 M Street, NW, Suite 400, Washington, D.C. 20036
www.pflag.org

PFLAG promotes the health and well-being of gay,

lesbian, bisexual, and transgendered persons, their families, and their friends through support to cope with an adverse society; education to enlighten an ill-informed public; and advocacy to end discrimination and secure equal civil rights.

George Leger's organization: **PROJECT ONLY A CHILD**
781-891-1730
18 Wadsworth Avenue, Waltham, MA 02453
www.onlyachild.org

Created in 1994, when George traveled to Guatemala to help homeless children, Only a Child is now an extensive outreach program. It serves upward of fifty youths and operates a shelter around the clock for those seeking to leave the street. Its carpentry shop is run and managed by the kids.

Kiaran Honderich's work: **ULALO**
www.purevisual.com/ulalo

Based in Boston, Ulalo builds connections between Americans and rural African women fighting AIDS. It works to illuminate the economic as well as the social and political causes of the AIDS pandemic and to strengthen the voices of the Africans who are fighting back.

Diane Wilson's inspiration: Unreasonable Women
   for the Earth!
www.unreasonablewomen.org
   In a 2002 speech to Bioneers (www.bioneers.org),
Diane Wilson concluded with this adaptation of a George
Bernard Shaw statement: "A reasonable woman adapts to
the world, an unreasonable woman makes the world
adapt to her. What this world needs is more unreasonable
women!" Her words and extraordinary achievements
triggered an electric reaction among the women present.
From that moment emerged an international network of
women supporting one another to take bold action based
on their values and vision of healing the earth.

Helping People Learn to Transform Conflict into Creative Action

Academy for the Love of Learning
928-203-4949
1725 West Highway 89A, Suite 6, Sedona, AZ 86336
www.aloveoflearning.org
   Conceived by Frankie's friend Aaron Stern and
famed musician Leonard Bernstein, the academy draws
upon the metaphor of music and its inner creative
tension between consonance and dissonance at the core

of its programming. Among its offerings is Leading by Being, personal-leadership training for change agents—consultants, artists, educators, social entrepreneurs, and those who wish to embrace and assist others in embracing the fullness of our human experience.

Jeff's work: **EDUCATORS FOR SOCIAL RESPONSIBILITY**
617-492-1764
23 Garden Street, Cambridge, MA 02138
www.esrnational.org

ESR helps educators create safe, caring, respectful, and productive learning environments. It also helps educators work with young people to develop the social skills, emotional competencies, and qualities of character they need to succeed in school and become contributing members of their communities.

Herb Walter's organization: **RURAL SOUTHERN VOICE FOR PEACE/THE LISTENING PROJECT**
828-675-5933
1036 Hannah Branch Road, Burnsville, NC 28714
www.listeningproject.info

An organizing tool for nonviolent social change that trains volunteers to conduct one-on-one interviews addressing local and sometimes national or international issues. Interviewers take time to build trust and understanding so that the interviewees can go deeper into their fears, hurts, hopes, needs, feelings, and ideas. You can request Listening Project trainers to work with your organization. The process takes four months to a year, and the results can be transformative.

Words to Embolden

It is not because things are difficult that we do not dare,
it is because we do not dare that things are difficult.

—Seneca

Fear is a natural reaction to moving closer to the truth.

—Pema Chödrön

I have not ceased being fearful, but I have ceased to let
fear control me. I have accepted fear as a part of life,
specifically the fear of change, the fear of the unknown,
and I have gone ahead despite the pounding in my heart
that says: turn back, turn back, you'll die if you venture
too far.

—Erica Jong

Solitude is a silent storm that breaks down all our dead branches; yet it sends our living roots deeper into the living heart of the living earth. —Kahlil Gibran

And the day came,
when the risk
to remain tight
in a bud
was more painful
than the risk
it took
to Blossom.
—Anaïs Nin

A most insidious form of fear is that which masquerades as common sense or even wisdom, condemning as foolish, reckless, insignificant, or futile the small, daily acts of courage which help to preserve man's self-respect and inherent human dignity.

—Daw Aung San Suu Kyi

To dare is to lose one's footing momentarily. To not dare is to lose oneself. —Søren Kierkegaard

I was going to die, if not sooner then later, whether or not I had ever spoken myself. My silences had not protected me. Your silence will not protect you.

—AUDRE LORDE

Courage is not the absence of fear, but rather the judgment that something else is more important than fear.

—AMBROSE REDMOON

What is needed, rather than running away or controlling or suppressing or any other resistance, is understanding fear; that means watch it, learn about it, come directly into contact with it. We are to learn about fear, not how to escape from it.   —JIDDU KRISHNAMURTI

Avoiding danger is no safer in the long run than outright exposure. Life is either a daring adventure, or nothing.

—HELEN KELLER

Our deepest fear is not that we are inadequate. Our deepest fear is that we are powerful beyond measure. It is our light, not our darkness, that most frightens us. . . . As we let our own light shine, we unconsciously give other people permission to do the same. As we are liberated from our own fear, our presence automatically liberates others.   —MARIANNE WILLIAMSON

Acknowledgments

From both of us: Our gratitude first to two people who made special contributions to this project—Dennis Burke, for his creativity and assistance in research and interviewing; and Anna Lappé, who cheerfully engaged her substantial insight, talent, and great energy to edit, fact-check, and develop the next-steps section that closes our book. Our thank-you also goes to our terrific agent, James Levine, for encouragement and help; as well as to our energetic, insightful Tarcher colleagues, publisher Joel Fotinos, executive editor Mitch Horowitz, and publicity manager Kelly Groves.

From Frankie: Given the nature of this book, it's only appropriate that I first acknowledge the skeptic—Dick Rowe, your doubt about our concept from the beginning, your probing questions, kept me open and struggling, unable to settle in before we had it right. I treasure your support, Dick, always arriving in the inimitable manner I love. I also know that it is in large measure because of the love of my children and friends— Peter Barnes, Hathaway Barry, Diana Beliard, Anne Black, Sylvia Blanchet, Mary Ann Carlson, Andrea Diehl, Mark Finser, Derrick Jensen, Bruce Kaiper, Susan Kanaan, Paul Lacey, Anthony and Anna Lappé, Josh Mailman, Nancy Moorehead, Linda Pritzker, Aaron Stern, Ginny Straus, Carol and Monroe Whitaker, and other dear ones—that I've been able to turn my fears into lessons I am able to share. Thank each of you for making this book possible.

From Jeff: First I want to thank my mentor, friend, and coauthor, Frankie, who provided inspiration for my vocation and patient guidance throughout the process of writing a first book. I owe so much to the support of my parents, John and Carol, and my sisters, Jane and Jennifer. I love you. Thanks also to the curious minds community for your inspiration and encouragement, especially Donnie Baker, Emily Frank, Jeannette Herrmann, Jeanne Hillson, Kiaran Honderich, Mia Howard, Dean Lampros, Mark Pettengill, Nina Selvaggio, Josh Silverman, and Alison Streit. My deep gratitude also goes to my friends and colleagues who provided essential support, especially Mitch Bogen, Robin Chalfin, Sunu Chandy, Caroline Chauncey, Larry Dieringer, Kirsten Giebutowski, Diane Gregorio, Lisa Groves, Carolyn Lambert, Carol Miller Lieber, Martha Plotkin, Jason Rand, Hector Risemberg, Laura Parker Roerden, and Sridhar Venkatapuram. And finally to Erich Goetzel, for our energetic conversations over many late-night dinners that challenged me to better understand both the possibilities and limits of facing our dragons.

Endnotes

1. Rainer Maria Rilke, *Letters to a Young Poet* trans. Stephen Mitchell (New York: Modern Library, 1984, 2001), 92.
2. See, for example, "State of Food Insecurity in the World 2002" (Food and Agriculture Organization of the United Nations, 2002), 1.
3. See, for example, Professor Joel Schwartz, Harvard University School of Public Health, "Harvesting and Long Term Exposure Effects in the Relations Between Air Pollution and Mortality," *American Journal of Epidemiology,* March 1, 2000 440–48: "Air pollution kills about 70,000 Americans each year. . . ."
4. See, for example, Mark Skousen, "Economics for the 21st Century," *Ideas on Liberty: Economics on Trial,* January 2000. Viewable at www.mskousen.com.
5. Madeleine K. Albright, "Bridges, Bombs, or Bluster?," *Foreign Affairs,* September/October 2003 www.foreignaffairs.org. The full quote is: "At some point we may be the only ones left. That's okay with me. We are America." See also Benjamin Barber, *Fear's Empire* (New York: W. W. Norton, 2003), 67.
6. Renana Brooks, "A Nation of Victims: Decoding Bush's Language of Power and Domination," *The Nation,* June 30, 2003. www.thenation.com.
7. Quoted from a televised interview with televangelist Jim Bakker in 1980. See comment quoted in, for instance, "Armageddon

Theology and Presidential Decision-Making: Religious Leaders' Concern," transcript of a press conference for religious issues 1984, in association with Conference on the Fate of the Earth and Washington Research Center, October 24, 1984, San Francisco Press Club.

8. Joseph Cirincione, *Deadly Arsenals: Tracking Weapons of Mass Destruction* (New York: Carnegie Endowment for Peace, June 2002).

9. Keith Bradsher, *High and Mighty: SUVs: The World's Most Dangerous Vehicles and How They Got That Way* (New York: Public Affairs, 2002).

10. Ibid., 97 and 96.

11. Ibid., 99.

12. Barry Glassner, *The Culture of Fear: Why Americans Are Afraid of the Wrong Things* (New York: Basic Books, 2000). See especially "Introduction: Why Americans Fear the Wrong Things."

13. Ibid.

14. "Report: Pollution Killing Thousands," CBSNews, August 16, 2001.

15. Berkeley Media Studies Group and Justice Policy Institute, "Off Balance: Youth, Race, and Crime in the News" (Washington, D.C.: Building Blocks for Youth, 2001).

16. Glassner, *The Culture of Fear*, 198.

17. Natalie Angier, "Why We're So Nice: We're Wired to Cooperate," *The New York Times*, July 23, 2002.

18. See David Niven, *The 100 Simple Secrets of Happy People: What Scientists Have Learned and How You Can Use It* (San Francisco: HarperSan Francisco, 2000), 2, quoting "In Pursuit of Happiness and Satisfaction in Later Life: A Study of Competing Theories of Subjective Well-Being," H. Lepper, Ph.D. thesis, University of California, Riverside.

19. The World Health Report 2001, Mental Health: New Understanding, New Hope. Message from Director-General. Viewed at www.who.int.whr2001.

20. Frances Moore Lappé and Anna Lappé, *Hope's Edge: The Next*

Diet for a Small Planet (New York: J. P. Tarcher/Penguin, 2002). For more information, see www.hopesedge.com.

21. On average, Americans have the television set on seven hours a day and watch it for four hours a day. See, for example, Todd Gitlin, *Media Unlimited: How the Torrent of Images and Sounds Overwhelms Our Lives* (New York: Henry Holt, 2002). See also fact sheets from TV Turnoff Week at www.tvturnoff.org.

22. "Astronomers Unveil First Detection of Dark Matter Object in the Milky Way," University of California, San Diego, Lawrence Livermore National Laboratory, news release, December 5, 2001.

23. Theodore Zeldin, *An Intimate History of Humanity* (New York: Random House, 1994), 197.

24. Ibid., 180.

25. Michael Clarkson, *Intelligent Fear: How to Make Fear Work for You* (Toronto: Key Porter Books, 2002), 24.

26. Jiddu Krishnamurti, *Freedom from the Known* (London: Victor Gollancz, Ltd., 1977), 46.

27. Visit the website at http://www.stanford.edu/~valarie.

28. Edmund L. Andrews, "Rich Nations Criticized for Barriers to Trade," *The New York Times,* September 9, 2002.

29. Rick Lazio, "Some Trade Barriers Won't Fall," *The New York Times,* August 9, 2003.

30. Actually, we learned later that Woody was more conservative than we are: His actual statement was "Eighty percent of success is just showing up," www.gadflyonline.com/10-1-01/film-woodyal-lenjunket.html

31. See, for example, Claudia Kalb, "Coping with Anxiety," *Newsweek,* February 24, 2003; Deborah Lott, "Unlearning Fear: Calcium Channel Blockers and the Process of Extinction," *Psychiatric Times,* May 2003, 9–12; Mohammed R. Milad and Gregory J. Quirk, "Neurons in Medial Prefrontal Cortex Signal Memory for Fear Extinction," *Nature* 420, November 7, 2002, 70–74; M. Davis et al, "Role of the Amygdala in Fear Extinction," *Annals of New York Academy of Sciences* 985:218–32, April 2003.

32. Linda Kulman, "Musings on Life and Limbs," *U.S. News & World*

Report, August 11, 2003. See also *Ambulance Girl: How I Saved Myself by Becoming an EMT* (New York: Crown, 2003).

33. Rush W. Dozier, Jr., *Fear Itself: The Origin and Nature of the Powerful Emotion That Shapes Our Lives and Our World* (New York: St. Martin's, 1998), 224.

34. Aung San Suu Kyi, *Freedom from Fear* (New York: Penguin, 1991), 180.

35. Examples include the Industrial Areas Foundation (www.iafnw. com); the Gamaliel Foundation (www.gamaliel.org); the Pacific Institute for Community Organizing (www.piconetwork.org). Large secular citizen organizations include ACORN—Association of Community Organizations for Reform Now (www.acorn.org).

36. See, for instance, the work of Educators for Social Responsibility at www.esrnational.org.

37. Viktor Frankl, *Man's Search for Ultimate Meaning* (Cambridge, Mass.: Perseus Publishing, 2000), 32. First published in 1948. The Jaspers quotation is also from Frankl, 32.

38. Eighty-five thousand refers to chemicals in commercial use. For more information about cancer and the environment, see fact sheets at the National Resources Defense Council, www.nrdc.org.

39. According to the Environmental Protection Agency in 2002, chemicals pose an elevated cancer risk to two-thirds of Americans living in nearly every part of the country. A study based on 1996 data of health risks from thirty-two toxic chemicals concluded that two hundred million people live in areas where the cancer risk from exposure to these substances is higher than what the EPA considers a minimum level of concern. See, for instance, "The Toxic Air We Breathe," CBSNews, June 1, 2002.

40. "Only a small proportion of the cases are accounted for by known risk factors, indicating the need for further research," from National Institutes of Health, National Cancer Institute, "Cancer: Rates and Risks," breast cancer section by Celia Byrne, Ph.D. Viewed at http://seer.cancer.gov/publications/raterisk/ riskstoc.html.

41. Op cit., Frankl, *Man's Search for Meaning,* 165.

42. Ibid., 133.

43. Charles Darwin, *The Descent of Man and Selection in Relation to Sex* (New York: D. Appleton, 1909), 121.

44. Naomi Eisenberger, Matthew Lieberman, University of California at Los Angeles; Kipling Williams, Macquarie University, Sydney, "Does Rejection Hurt? An MRI study of Social Exclusion," *Science Magazine,* Oct. 10, 2003.

45. David Grossman, *On Killing: The Psychological Cost of Learning to Kill in War and Society* (Boston: Little, Brown, 1995), 150.

46. Ethel S. Person, *Feeling Strong* (New York: Quill, 2003), 268–82.

47. Warren Bennis and Patricia Ward Biederman, *Organizing Genius: The Secrets of Creative Collaboration* (Cambridge, Mass.: Perseus Publishing, 1998), 5–6.

48. Steven Johnson, *Emergence: The Connected Lives of Ants, Brains, Cities, and Software* (New York: Touchstone/Simon & Schuster, 2002), 198–99.

49. Ransom A. Myers and Boris Worm, "Rapid Worldwide Depletion of Predatory Fish Communities," *Nature* 423, 280–83, May 15, 2003.

50. Rebecca Solnit, "Acts of Hope: Challenging Empire on the World Stage," *OrionOnline,* 2003. Viewable at www.oriononline.org.

51. William McDonough and Michael Braungert, *Cradle to Cradle: Remaking the Way We Make Things* (New York: North Point Press, 2002), 17.

52. Antonio Damasio, *Looking for Spinoza: Joy, Sorrow, and the Feeling Brain* (New York: Harcourt, 2003), 160–61, citing Robert Miller et al. "The Communication of Affect in Monkeys: Cooperative Conditions," *Journal of Genetic Psychology* 108, 1966. See also Robert Miller, "Experimental Approaches to the Physiological and Behavioral Concomitants of Affective Communication in Rhesus Monkeys," in Stuart A. Altmann, ed., *Social Communication Among Primates* (Chicago: University of Chicago Press, 1967).

53. Allan Luks with Peggy Payne, *The Healing Power of Doing Good:*

The Health and Spiritual Benefits of Helping Others (New York: Ballantine Books, 1992), see: "Chapter Two: Helper's High: The First Phase."

54. Lee Clark, "Panic: Myth or Reality," *Contexts Magazine,* Fall 2002. See also www.leeclark.com.

55. Clark McPhail, "Stereotypes of Crowds and Collective Behavior: Looking Backward, Looking Forward," in Dan Miller, Michael Katovich, and Stanley Saxton, eds., *Constructing Complexity: Symbolic Interaction and Social Forms* (Greenwich, Conn.: JAI Press, 1997).

56. Rushmore Kidder, *Shared Values for a Troubled World: Conversations with Women and Men of Conscience* (New York: Simon & Schuster, 1994).

57. Adam Smith, *The Theory of Moral Sentiments* (Indianapolis: Liberty Classics, 1982), D. D. Raphael and A. L. Macfie, eds., pt. 1, sec.2. ch 1, 80, 86.

58. Sarah F. Brosnan and Frans B. M. de Waal, "Monkeys Reject Unequal Pay," *Nature,* 423, September 18, 2003.

59. Damasio, *Looking for Spinoza,* 160.

60. Albert-László Barabási, *Linked: How Everything Is Connected to Everything Else and What It Means for Business, Science, and Everyday Life* (New York: Penguin/Plume, 2002), 7.

61. Ibid., 12.

62. Ibid.

63. "Estimates show that up to 70 percent of the 2 million nongovernmental organizations in the United States have been created in the last three decades. The number of nongovernmental organizations operating internationally—those with a significant presence in three or more countries—has quadrupled to 20,000 in that same period" (WorldWatch Institute). Curtis Runyan, "Action on the Front Lines," *World Watch,* November/December 1999. See also www.worldwatch.org.

64. Between 1989 and 1998, the number went from 464,002 to 734,000. "Number of Tax-exempt Organizations Registered with

the IRS, 1989–1998," Urban Institute, National Center for Charitable Statistics, 1998 (www.nccs.urban.org).

65. Frances Moore Lappé and Paul Martin Du Bois, *The Quickening of America* (San Francisco: Jossey-Bass, 1994).

66. James Gorman, "Contrary to Orwell, Democracy Rules on the Big Animal Farm, *The New York Times,* January 14, 2003.

67. Rupert Sheldrake, *The Sense of Being Stared At: And Other Aspects of the Extended Mind* (New York: Crown, 2003).

68. Rainer Maria Rilke, *Letters to a Young Poet,* trans. Stephen Mitchell (New York: Modern Library, 1984–2001), 34–35.

Index

About the Authors

Frances Moore Lappé became a public figure upon the 1971 release of *Diet for a Small Planet*. The thirtieth-anniversary sequel, *Hope's Edge: The Next Diet for a Small Planet*, coauthored with her daughter, Anna, was released by Tarcher/Penguin in 2002. Jane Goodall described it as "absolutely one of the most important books as we move into the twenty-first century." Lappé, a sought-after public speaker, has appeared on hundreds of radio and television programs, including the *Today* show. Her articles and opinion pieces have been published in venues from *The New York Times* to *Reader's Digest* to *Harper's*; profiles have appeared in such publications as *The Boston Globe Magazine, People,* and *Utne*. A documentary on her life's work aired on Australian and British television. Lappé has authored or coauthored fourteen books and is the cofounder of two national organizations, including the thirty-year-old California-based Institute for Food and Development Policy, better known as Food First. A former visiting scholar at the Massachusetts Institute of Technology, Lappé has received sixteen honorary doctoral degrees from distinguished institutions, including the University of Michigan, Kenyon College, and Notre Dame. In 1987 she became the fourth American to receive the Right Livelihood Award, often called the "Alternative Nobel." In 2003 she was chosen as one of fifty people by artist Robert Shetterly for his photography exhibition, "Americans Who Tell the Truth." Contact her at www.smallplanetinstitute.org (website) or frances@smallplanetinstitute.org (e-mail).

Jeffrey Perkins is the cofounder of curious minds, a Boston-based network supporting people who want to clarify and move into their life's work. Jeff facilitates life transitions for groups and individuals and conducts Fear Means Go workshops, based on ideas in this book. During the 1990s, Jeff was the executive coordinator for Frances Moore Lappé's Center for Living Democracy, where he helped launch its national-solutions-oriented newswire, the American News Service. He has worked in social-change organizations for ten years, in such fields as citizen democracy, education, and political organizing, most recently at Educators for Social Responsibility in Cambridge, Massachusetts. Jeff earned his master's degree in American Studies from the University of Massachusetts, Boston, and his BA in peace and global studies and politics from Earlham College in Richmond, Indiana. Jeff can be reached at www.curiousminds.org (website) or jeff@curiousminds.org (e-mail).